PRAISE FOR JOHN LEWIS

"Generations from now when parents teach their children what is meant by courage, the story of John Lewis will come to mind. His life is a lesson in the fierce urgency of now."

—PRESIDENT BARACK OBAMA,
from his Medal of Freedom remarks

"We have in John Lewis a moral force for good. In this book he presents a gift: the story of a loving American hero, and how we can become that too. Here is a snapshot of Lewis' faith in action."

—DOUGLAS BRINKLEY, #1 *New York Times* bestselling
author of *Rosa Parks* and *The Reagan Diaries*

"In John Lewis, we are humbled to see a person of towering physical and moral courage—a man who has accomplished what so many others have dared to try."

—SENATOR EDWARD KENNEDY

"[John Lewis is] a genuine American hero and moral leader who commands widespread respect in the chamber."

—*ROLL CALL*

"John Lewis is the conscience of the U.S. Congress."

—ANDREW YOUNG, 14th United States
ambassador to the United Nations

"Thank you, John Lewis, for remaining a beacon of light in dark times." —*VOGUE*

ACROSS
THAT
BRIDGE

ACROSS THAT BRIDGE

A Vision for Change and the Future of America

CONGRESSMAN

JOHN LEWIS

WITH BRENDA JONES

hachette
BOOKS

NEW YORK   BOSTON

Hachette Books
Hachette Book Group
1290 Avenue of the Americas, New York, NY 10104
hachettebooks.com
twitter.com/hachettebooks

First Hardcover Edition: May 2012
First Trade Paperback Edition: August 2017

Hachette Books is a division of Hachette Book Group, Inc. The Hachette Books name and logo are trademarks of Hachette Book Group, Inc.

The publisher is not responsible for websites (or their content) that are not owned by the publisher.

The Hachette Speakers Bureau provides a wide range of authors for speaking events. To find out more, go to www.hachettespeakersbureau.com or call (866) 376-6591.

Print book interior design by Renato Stanisic.

Library of Congress Cataloging- in- Publication Data

Lewis, John, 1940 Feb. 21–
Across that bridge: a vision for change and the future of America/John Lewis.—1st ed.
p. cm.
ISBN 978- 1- 4013- 2411- 7
1. Lewis, John, 1940 Feb. 21—Philosophy. 2. Conduct of life. 3. Legislators—United States—Biography. 4. African American legislators—Biography. 5. United States. Congress. House—Biography. 6. Civil rights workers—United States—Biography. 7. African American civil rights workers—Biography. I. Title.
E840.8.L43A3 2012
328.73'092—dc23 2011050558

ISBNs: 978-0-316-51093-6 (paperback); 978-1-4013-2411-7 (hardcover); 978-1-4013-0374-7 (ebook)

Printed in the United States of America

LSC-C

10 9 8 7 6 5 4 3

To my wife, Lillian,

My parents, Eddie and Willie Mae Lewis,

and all the builders of the Beloved Community

CONTENTS

Contents

ACROSS
THAT
BRIDGE

INTRODUCTION

*"Some men see things as they are and say 'Why?' I dream
things that never were and say 'Why not?'"*
—ROBERT F. KENNEDY

I have written these lessons on freedom and meditations on
change for the generations who will take us into the future,
for the dreamers young and ever young who should never get
lost in a sea of despair, but are faithfully readying themselves
for the next push for change. It is for the parents who want to
inspire their sons and daughters to build a more just society.
And, it's for the sons and daughters who hear the call of a new
age.

This book is for the people. It is for the grassroots leaders
who will emerge not for the sake of fame or fortune, but with
a burning desire to do good. It is for all those willing to join

in the human spirit's age-old struggle to break free from the bondage of concepts and structures that have lost their use. It is for the masses of people who with each new day have the chance to peel the scales from their eyes and remember it is they alone who are the most powerful agents of change. It is for anyone who wants to reform his or her existence or to fashion a better life for the children. It's for those who want to improve their community or make their mark in history. This book is a collection of a few of the truths that I have learned as one who dreamed, worked, and struggled in America's last revolution.

Some people have told me that I am a rare bird in the blue sky of dreamers. I believed innocently and profoundly as a child that the world could be a better place. Most visionaries are born so ahead of their time, they must sequester themselves in the world of poetry or philosophy to express what they hope to see. I was a child with high ideals, lucky enough to have been born in an age when the wave of social transformation was about to culminate into the most powerful nonviolent movement for change in American history. I have survived the worst aggression, all the attacks mounted against dreamers to stamp out the light that they see. I have been rejected, hated, oppressed, beaten, jailed, and have almost died only to live another day. I have witnessed betrayal, corruption, bombing, lunacy, conspiracy, and even assassination—and I have still kept marching on. And despite every attempt to keep me down, I have not been shaken. I held on to my mind and my faith so that today I am blessed to actually see so many of the changes in this world that we dreamed would take shape. And now I can share what got me through, my guiding philosophy, so that anyone feeling victimized by peers or impatient with our government, offended by the inequities of our economy, or wondering about the road to success, will be inspired.

We have come a great distance as a society, but we still have a great distance to go. The progress we take for granted today brought on by the successes of the modern-day Civil Rights Movement is just one more step down a very long road toward the realization of our spiritual destiny as a nation of "freedom and justice for all." There is still much more work to do. One movement will never offer all the growth humanity needs to experience. To expect so is to build your hopes on a puff of smoke, on a whispered breath; it is to anticipate an illusion. Remember how we thought the election of President Obama meant we had finally created a postracial America, a place where the problems that have haunted us for so long were finally silenced? Nobody says that anymore. We no longer dwell in that daydream. We were shaken to realism by the harshness of what we have witnessed in the last few years—the vilification of President Obama, a drive to wreck his legacy and undo the progress we have made as a nation in the last hundred years, a disdain for the sick and the poor, militarization of the police, and the weaponizing of government not to serve as an advocate, but as an agent of oppression and compliance. We have seen the suicide of Kalief Browder, who died trying to defend his innocence in a system that could only see his guilt; the deaths of Trayvon Martin; Michael Brown; Freddie Gray; and scores of black and brown men and women, where few to none are held accountable. We have seen the rise of hate groups in America, murder at the Holocaust Museum, the mass deportation of immigrants, the harassment and murder of Muslims.

Political parties are on the hunt to search and destroy each other, as though we were involved in some kind of enemy combat, rather than the work of statesmanship. Campaigns have become a free-for-all of dirty tricks, scandalmongering, and distracting negativity that obscures the people's need to examine a candidate's voting record and see where he or she actually stands on the issues. I find myself asking my colleagues today, "Why do we have to be so mean? Is there something in the air we breathe or the water we drink that incites us to bring one another down, to violate one another with so much glee?"

President Obama was called a liar during a joint session of Congress at a State of the Union Address. It was probably the lowest point of decorum I have witnessed in more than twenty years in the Congress. A campaign volunteer aggressively subdued a woman and stomped on her head prior to a 2010 senatorial debate in Kentucky. The woman, who was holding a satirical sign, had approached the candidate she opposed for a photo. The campaign volunteer said he acted to protect the candidate, but commentators speculated that he was enraged by the woman's sign. Regardless of the cause, the assault, which was caught on video, was shocking. Ironically, the abuser went on to demand an apology from the victim, saying, "I would like for her to apologize to me, to be honest with you." But once we witnessed this kind of tragedy, it seemed we had not had enough. In the next national election the intolerance of difference got even worse. It became a rallying cry couched in code words—"Make America Great Again"—as though diversity had damaged not uplifted our civilization.

Even I, who has looked down the barrel of a gun with only my faith to defend me, would say there is a unique hostility in these times that almost seems worse to me than what we experienced in the 1960s. It is true, we were confronted with state-sponsored brutality, and people died because of the complicity of local government with fearmongering and terror. Yet, in those days, we could look to federal authority as a sympathetic referee in the struggle for civil rights and as an advocate for the need to challenge injustice.

The water crisis in Flint, Michigan occurred not because of corporate interests, but because of an abuse of the public trust. Why the local government took these risks has not become clear. Today it seems there is no moral basis for anything we do as a society. Even raising the idea of what is good or what is best is seen as an irrelevant burden to any debate. There was a time when politicians needed to be great orators because the people themselves were grappling with the challenges of conscience, trying to perceive what is "right" and what is "wrong." But to-day, not only do we miss the eloquence of public speaking, but the moral compass of so many leaders seems to be skewed.

It's taken a long time, but finally the people are awakening to the truth: the truth of their responsibility for the democratic process. Finally they are realizing they can never afford to relegate their power to representatives in a system that offers every citizen the power to vote. The Goliath has finally remembered its strength and its duty. The people are gathering their forces, reengaging, and applying pressure.

I have seen this restlessness among the people before. It was in another millennium, another decade, and at another time in our history, but it pushed through America like a storm. In ten short years, there was a tempest that transformed what the American Revolution did not address, what the Constitution and the Bill of Rights were afraid to confront, what the Civil

War could not unravel, what Reconstruction tried to mediate, and Jim Crow did its best to retrench. This mighty wind made a fundamental shift in the moral character of our nation that has reached every sector of our society. And this history lends us one very powerful reminder today: Nothing can stop the power of a committed and determined people to make a difference in our society. Why? Because human beings are the most dynamic link to the divine on this planet. Governments and corporations do not live. They have no power, no capacity in and of themselves. They are given life and derive all their authority from their ability to assist, benefit, and transform the lives of the people they touch. All authority emanates from the consent of the governed and the satisfaction of the customer. Somehow it seems leaders have forgotten this fundamental principle, and we must right ourselves before the people withdraw their support.

As a disenfranchised citizen who yearned for change, as a child born on the dark side of the American dream, I heard the whispers of the spirit calling me to wrestle with the soul of a nation. I could see a higher vision of what this nation could be, and I can say to every leader who might be entangled in the web of the status quo that when the people are ready, this nation will change. Whenever the people finally reject the efforts to fragment their collective energies into warring factions and remember their divine union with one another, when they throw off material distractions and irrelevant negativity and hear their souls speak with one voice, they will rise up. And whatever is in their path will either transform or transpire.

During the Civil Rights Movement, our struggle was not about politics. It was about seeing a philosophy made manifest in our society that recognized the inextricable connection we have to each other. Those ideals represent what is eternally real and they are still true today, though they have receded from the forefront of American imagination. Yes, the election of Obama represented a significant step, but, as the following presidential election and all the days beyond that high point in American history have proved, it was not an ending. It was not even a beginning; it was one important step on a continuum of change. It was a major down payment on the fulfillment of a dream. It was another milestone on our nation's road to freedom. But we must accept one central truth as participants in a democracy: Freedom is not a state; it is an act. It is not some enchanted garden perched high on a distant plateau where we can finally sit down and rest. Freedom is the continuous action we all must take, and each generation must do its part to create an even more fair, more just society. The work of love, peace, and justice will always be necessary, until their realism and their imperative takes hold of our imagination, crowds out any dream of hatred or revenge, and fills up our existence with their power.

It is my hope the leaders of today will heed the warning the people have so patiently tendered and shake off the shackles of inertia. Let us remove the false burdens of partisanship, personal ambition, and greed, and begin to do the work we were all appointed to do to move this country forward. Let us appeal to our similarities, to the higher standards of integrity, decency, and the common good, rather than to our differences, be they age, gender, sexual preference, class, or color. If not, the people will put aside the business of their lives and turn their attention to the change they are determined to see, just as the Women's March, Black Lives Matter, the Equal Justice Initiative, the Coalition of Immokalee Workers, and others so adamantly demonstrate. The international scope of these efforts and the widespread connections created by the Internet suggest that people are beginning to see that their relationship to one another is greater than the differences of borders, culture, and language. People are beginning to see that what happens in Asia affects trading on Wall Street, and what breeds conflict in Africa is a commentary on lifestyles in Europe, and what is created in India or China is consumed by the people in Latin America. They are beginning to awaken to an idea we gave meaning to in the sixties: We are one people, one family, the human family, and what affects one of us affects us all.

I will never forget the morning of the March on Washington in August 1963. I, along with so many others, had had enough. Our people had been waiting nearly four hundred years and would not take no for an answer any longer. We were going to do all we could to move our society to a place where it recognized our inherent right to be counted.

Washington had been tense in preparation for the largest convergence of black people the city had ever seen. So, before we started, my colleagues and I, the "Big Six" leaders of the Civil Rights Movement, paid a courtesy visit to Capitol Hill to speak with members of Congress. There was great concern about keeping order and peace during the march. But, when our quick series of meetings with House and Senate leaders was over, something amazing happened. We stepped outside the congressional buildings into the light of day and saw thousands in the streets. The people had started the march without us! They had heard the call to nonviolent action; they had taken the reins and were on the move together, peacefully making their point. We were technically the "leaders," but our duty at that moment was to follow. The people were marching to the voice of one spirit that was uniting them to work for change through the power of peace, and I couldn't have been more proud.

What is the purpose of a nation if not to empower human beings to live better together than they could individually? When government fails to meet the basic needs of humanity for food, shelter, clothing, and even more important—the room to grow and evolve—the people will begin to rely on one another, to pool their resources and rise above the artificial limitations of tradition or law. Each of us has something significant to contribute to society be it physical, material, intellectual, emotional, or spiritual. Each of us is born for a reason, to serve a divine purpose. If the structures of our lives do not contribute to that purpose or if they complicate our ability to live, to be free and to be happy, or even worse, if they lead to the confines of oppression, then we seek change, sometimes radical change, even revolution, to satisfy the yearning of our souls.

If we believe in the divine essence of all human life, then we must allow that the same essential spirit rests at the core of all our collective action, including the work of government, as well as the action of protest. The collective power of the people is not only a material, emotional, and economic resource, but it is a spiritual force as well. As we look back on our national story we can see many accounts of "man's unending search for freedom," as President Lyndon Johnson once put it. It is a struggle not only against the oppression imposed by human beings on one another, but it is an inner struggle of the American soul to free itself from the contradictions of its own fallacies about the nature of true democracy, freedom, and equality. In our individual lives we grow through learning from our mistakes. As a nation we evolve by contending with the consequences of our decisions to reach that point where the collective mind is not tempted by injustice. Those of my philosophical framework call this process "building a Beloved Community." We defined it as a society based on simple justice that values the dignity and the worth of every human being. When we arrive at the place where we as a people live in the light of that kind of consciousness, then we will have reached a point where we can finally put down the burdens of hate, violence, and division. Until that day, struggle is inevitable because tension motivates the imperative to change.

The restless call for change blew constantly through my mind and disturbed my peace as a boy growing up in the cotton fields of Alabama. I was like a little wisp of dust wafting in a sea of adversity, a black boy trying to get the kind of education that would lead to better opportunity crashing against the rock-hard heart of the Jim Crow South. That was a bitter, harsh experience that made me feel as though the world was set against me. I think that is how some people feel today struggling against the worst economic odds we have seen in eighty years, losing their homes, their jobs, and their pensions. They can't seem to get ahead. The deck seems persistently stacked against them.

I understand the sense of helplessness and hopelessness that can surround a people who feel thwarted at every turn. I could not have been farther away from the halls of Congress or the chambers of the Supreme Court as a small boy in Alabama. Back then I could not choose my seat on a bus or sit down at a lunch counter to eat, and blacks certainly didn't have the access to vote. No provision had been made for me and others like me to communicate the dictates of our conscience to the leadership of a nation. We had to build that road ourselves. We made a way out of no way to free ourselves from oppression and bring an American society one step closer to realizing its pledge: "one nation, indivisible, with liberty and justice for all."

———————

"The difference between what we do and what we are capable of doing would suffice to solve most of the world's problems."
—MOHANDAS GANDHI

Each generation must continue to struggle and begin where the last left off. The sprouting of activist groups and angry sentiments represents a growing sense of discontent in America and around the world. These human beings represent a growing feeling of dissatisfaction that the community of nations is spending the people's resources on more bombs, missiles, and guns and not enough on human needs. People are crying out. They want to see the governments of the world's nations humanize their policies and practices. They want to see business leaders and their corporations be more humane and more concerned about the problems that affect the whole of the world's population, rather than just the overrepresented rich.

Some activists today may not seem as focused, prepared, or organized as we were in the Civil Rights Movement, but they are getting there. Every successful movement needs to have achievable goals to give the people involved some victories. That keeps them focused, keeps them going.

I cannot predict what kind of change will come. I cannot offer marching orders for a new band of liberators. But I can boil down some of what I know into an essence that can be molded into the structures that you will ultimately create. That is why this little book is divided into a collection of truths that I have discovered are fundamental to the inner transformation that must be realized to affect lasting social change. I have gleaned these ideas from my own formative experiences, from time spent in the crucible that created a new America, and from the challenges of today. I literally grew up sitting-in and sitting down in protest, on the frontlines of the struggle for social justice in America, and it is my hope that when you read this, you will take away ideas that will encourage you to take action in your own lives and in our world.

The most important lesson I have learned in the fifty years I have spent working toward the building of a better world is that the true work of social transformation starts within. It begins inside your own heart and mind, because the battle-ground of human transformation is really, more than any other thing, the struggle within the human consciousness to believe and accept what is true. Thus to truly revolutionize our society, we must first revolutionize ourselves. We must be the change we seek if we are to effectively demand transformation from others. It is clear that the pot is being stirred and people are beginning to breathe in the essences of change that will lead the soul to act. Who will emerge at the forefront of this struggle in the twenty-first century? Perhaps it will be you.

FAITH

Faith is the substance of things hoped for, the
evidence of things not seen.

HEBREWS 11:1

There is one question people ask me more than any other: How did you do it? How did you hold to nonviolence when a pounding wall of vicious hate was pushing through you like waves of fire during the protests and sit-ins of the Civil Rights Movement? How is it possible to be cracked on the head with a nightstick, left bleeding and unconscious on the trampled grass, and not raise your hand one time in self-defense? How could you bear the clear hypocrisy of being arrested on trumped-up charges and taken to jail for disturbing the peace when you were the one who was attacked and abused? How could you survive the unanswered threats, the bombings, and murders of a lineage of people, like Medgar Evers, Jimmie Lee Jackson, Andrew Goodman, James Chaney, and Michael

"Mickey" Schwerner, without holding any bitterness or anger? The answer is simple. Faith. Faith has the power to deliver us all, even from the greatest harm.

Faith, to me, is knowing in the solid core of your soul that the work is already done, even as an idea is being conceived in your mind. It is being as sure as you are about your dreams as you are about anything you know as a hard fact. For example, you are sure you know how to drive to your home from your job. No one could make you doubt that you know the way. You are sure that clouds drift in a light blue sky; you know the date you were born. Faith is being so sure of what the spirit has whispered in your heart that your belief in its eventuality is unshakable. Nothing can make you doubt that what you have heard will become a reality. Even if you do not live to see it come to pass, you know without one doubt that it will be. That is faith.

What Shakespeare wrote in *As You Like It* is not only poetic and beautiful, it also expresses a profound truth: "All the world's a stage," he says, "and all the men and women merely players." Life is like a drama, and any person who is truly committed to an ideal must believe in the authority of a divine plan. Not a rigid, micromanagement of human behavior that predicts every step of every individual, but a set of divine boundaries that governs the present, the past, and the future—a set of principles humankind does not have the capacity to override, no matter how far we attempt to stray from its dictates.

What we were communicating through nonviolent protest, what we were demonstrating by being willing to put our bodies on the line, was that love had already overcome hate, that the pages of America's book had already been written, that this nation's destiny was already sealed in the moment it was founded, so every expression of evil, including segregation, could never stand.

We were actors dramatizing our faith in the supremacy of one truth that no law, no centuries-old tradition, no military force, no material might, no matter how ferocious, could undermine the dictates of the divine. We knew the risks, because America had held so intensely to the false notion of inherent inequality that we as a nation believed it was real, and people believed their reality verified it as the truth. We knew people would even kill rather than disrupt the notion of inherent inequality. We knew we had to be prepared to accept the sacrifices of beating, arrests, and jail. It was our faith, our knowing with an iron-clad certainty, that held us in the midst of threats, bombings, and even when we faced the deaths of cherished, courageous, visionary members of the movement.

I had lived inside the irrationality of hatred and discrimination, and I had seen that it made no sense. I saw the dignity of the most American of virtues displayed all around my community in the actions of my family and friends. My parents, their parents before them, and my great-grandparents were hardworking, honest, humble, family-centered people. They had an innate intelligence that was unrecognized by society, and they used an inspiring creativity to survive, even thrive. They were good, plain and simple, undeserving of hate. I witnessed the necessary human interaction between blacks and whites—especially vital in farm life, which silently crossed those unreasonable social boundaries—where shades of mutual respect were imparted but kept in the dark out of fear.

Even as a boy I knew in my heart and soul that the equality of all humankind was not just a dream. Children growing up under inhumane conditions are not carefree. They sense that something is wrong and embark on an inner search to explain so much that is not in keeping with their hearts. At a young age, I mourned for the experience of a more loving world. My soul insisted there was a better way. Many of us who joined the struggle of respect for human dignity, both black and white, Protestant and Jew, had been locked in cognitive dissonance for years. By the time we were seasoned freedom fighters, it was more real to us than our own flesh and blood, more real than our own lives, and more valuable than our own longevity. We believed that if we are all children of the same Creator, then discrimination had to be an error, a misconception based on faulty logic. The idea that some people were inherently better was a delusion of the human ego, a distortion of the truth. We asserted our right to human dignity based on a solid faith in our divine heritage that linked us to every other human being and all the rest of creation, known and unknown, even to the heart and mind of God and the highest celestial realms in the universe.

This unity was an intrinsic, inseparable aspect of our being. We had nothing to prove. Our worth had already been established before we were born. Our protests were an affirmation of this faith, and our belief that we could never be separated from this truth. It did not matter that hundreds of years of unjust law and demeaning customs were tied to this wrongheaded thinking, or that the history of an entire nation had been shaped by this error in judgment. We believed that if we were the children of an omniscient Creator and we took a stand based on faith, that the forces of the universe would come to our aid. No jail cell, no threat, no act of violence could alter our power to overcome any adversary, if we did not waver.

Your faith has the power to sustain you through the worst that you can imagine. You may have heard this somewhere before in your life. Religious leaders teach about faith on holy days. You might read about it in self-help books, pop psychology, or spiritual literature. People pat you on the back when they know you are going through a hard time and encourage you to have faith as a way to comfort you. Few would disagree with the idea that faith has power, but often this truth does not become meaningful to us until we are tested by a challenge we think we may not survive. It is then that we experience how transformative our capacity to believe truly is.

Tragedy is the great equalizer, and no individual, regardless of wealth or fame, can escape the challenge tragedy brings. If one primary purpose in our lives is to cast off all illusions and awaken to the eternal knowledge of what is truly real, then tragedy can be viewed as an equal opportunity aid to our development. The problems we face in the trials of our lives, whether we are standing in protest against injustice or fighting cancer, battling addictions or bankruptcy, our problems can help each of us grow beyond our personal limits. Our problems initiate a struggle within our own souls that take us to the brink of our own experience. As we command our spirit to find a way to overcome these obstacles, we are forced to break past any false trappings of the identity, and to focus intensely on what is real, and what is truly important.

Mother Teresa was asked where she found her strength,
her focus, her fuel. The fuel, she explained, is prayer. "To keep
a lamp burning, we have to keep putting oil in it."

Have you ever considered that the same power you activate in the midst of adversity can also be consciously utilized to bring forward the kind of change or transformation you would like to see in your own life? In the Civil Rights Movement, we actively and consciously utilized the power of faith to move our society forward. We used faith as a shield against the false notion that anyone has the power to inflict pain, limitation, despair, or any condition upon us. We in the movement decided to actualize our belief that the hatred we experienced was not based on any truth, but was actually an illusion in the minds of those who hated us.

The struggle for civil rights was more than a series of legal battles. It was a spiritual confrontation that tested the power of two ideas—one based on unity and the other based on division. Our faith rejected the notion that some people were inherently better than others because of skin color, hair, height, build, education, class, or religion, or any external attribute, and it embraced the equality and divinity of all humanity. In the moment that we relaxed into full recognition of our connection to the Creator, we remembered the words: "no weapon formed against you shall prosper." When we cast off the false notions designed to limit us and twist our creative powers to serve the work of shame and fear, we began to step into the majesty of our faith. When we rejected the idea that we were powerless, worthless, and incapable of counteracting the force of an unjust government, we could feel our faith building and our strength gaining.

Many people misconstrue the motivation of Rosa Parks to keep her seat on the segregated bus in Montgomery. They have said that she was a seamstress simply tired on her way home from work, who decided that day she would not get up. But she herself would say that her longtime work as a secretary for the National Association for the Advancement of Colored People (NAACP) informed her of the organized actions already in motion to challenge the bus system. Her knowledge of a structured movement to resist was the foundation of her protest, but it was a course she took at Highlander Folk School in Monteagle, Tennessee, about six weeks before she began her protest, that took her off the sidelines and placed her at the center of the movement.

Highlander was an oasis for many that featured an engaging program focused on empowering the downtrodden and oppressed in Appalachia as well as Southerners, both black and white. Myles Horton, one of the founders of Highlander, made it his life's work to bring the principles of the Bible to bear on everyday life.

His early experiences made him begin to question why the church was not using the power of faith to answer the needs of the people around him in Appalachia. He felt the church was too often satisfied with platitudes and the memorization of sacred texts, while it remained silent on the moral, material, and even spiritual crises that people faced. The new theology he studied posited that faith should respond not only to the ethereal needs of humanity, but it should have a holistic impact on the lives of believers and on the communities in which they lived. If faith had power, he declared, then its ability should be challenged to answer even our physical and material concerns and not be reserved for religious services and activities. If faith had meaning, its benefits should accrue not only after death, but it should have the capacity to answer the cries of humanity here and now.

It was out of his compassion for the Appalachian families, born in the same mountains as he, that Horton created Highlander as an institution to educate mountain people, inform them of their rights, give them a central home to organize grassroots activism, and most important, to help restore their faith in themselves.

Highlander's early work was an outgrowth of the labor movement of the 1930s and '40s, but after the *Brown v. Board of Education* decision in 1954, Horton knew he would have to begin educating around the need for racial equality. So when Rosa Parks visited Highlander in the summer of 1955, she was immersed in an institution with a decades-long commitment to integration. Noted educators and activists emerged from the ranks of the teachers at Highlander, such as the renowned Septima Clark and Bernice Johnson Reagon, a historian well-known today as the founder of the *a capella* singing group called Sweet Honey in the Rock. Folk singers Guy Carawan and Pete Seeger were also Highlander regulars. Martin Luther King Jr. saw Highlander as a retreat, a place to rest and restore himself during the stressful height of the movement.

Parks heard about Highlander's workshops in desegregation and decided to attend a class there. She marveled at the team of integrated teachers who taught her and worked as equal partners in her instruction. The basis of their curriculum was spiritual, structured to remind the participants of the inherent divinity of all humankind, which meant every participant there was also a spark of the divine. Parks attributed one of the major reasons she decided to stay seated to a desire to test this freshly awakened understanding. She wanted to see if this faith had the potency to defend her against the lie of her inferiority, even though the whole society surrounding her was founded on that idea. And when the driver told her she would be arrested, perhaps you recall her words were, "You may do that." She was asserting her power over her own destiny, giving the driver permission to do what she was allowing him to do, not what he was forcing her to do.

She was declaring that as a child of the divine, she had a power that no other human being, regardless of their status, could ever take away. A policeman, a government, even a militia, or an angry mob bathed in the work of injustice only had the power to beat us, arrest us, or take us to jail. Our faith was that no force of humankind, no matter how brutal, could overcome the power of the divine. We believed that if we stood together as one people, gathered by our faith, determined to demonstrate the falsity of notions coursing through the society around us, then we would have heavenly protection against any evil that would befall us. We did not know how that help would come, but we knew it would come because the battle we were fighting had already been won. The truth had already been established. All we needed to do was call it forward and crash the illusions of injustice.

This surety of support came, for many of us, from living on the precarious edge of subsistence. In the movement, we had very little money, no political influence, no military force, and very few in the society around us believed in our capacity to contribute even the most basic of human gifts—to think with any clarity, to learn new things, to invent or create, to understand the world around us, or even to stand up to defend ourselves. We had no safety net, no one to turn to. We were born into the unfair circumstances that most people find themselves facing only temporarily at some point in their lives. We began stripped down to the bare minimum. We started out our lives dangling by a tenuous thread, so many of us came to the work of change already deeply experienced in the transformative power of faith. Our mothers and fathers had prayed us through the dire circumstances of living in the Deep South—poverty, hunger, grinding debt, a system of sharecropping stacked against us, illiteracy, limited educational opportunity, not to mention the terrorism of the nightriders and mob violence. So many of our parents stayed on their knees and made sure we learned to pray that we were already familiar with the power of divine grace that would meet us in our darkest hour and somehow, someway seemed to stretch the span of our universe to make two short ends meet. This was so much a part of our everyday lives that we had a name for it. We called it "making a way out of no way." So when we were standing in protest facing police dogs and fire hoses, we knew without any doubt that somebody who was greater than us all would make a way out of no way and protect the defenders of the truth.

The role of the church cannot be understated here, and you can expand the concept of church to mean the communion of believers. It has been well documented that the church was a wellspring of common faith for most of us in the movement. It was no accident that the movement was led primarily by ministers—not politicians, presidents, or even community activists—but ministers first, who believed they were called to the work of civil rights as an expression of their faith. Religious faith is a powerful connecting force for any group of people who are working toward social change. The common principles and structure of our beliefs linked people across racial, ethnic, regional, and economic differences who were hoping to contribute to this growing call for change. And the universal principles that all the great religions share, like the power of compassion and the mandate to practice one's faith, connected us beyond the boundaries of religious precept and joined Jews, Protestants, Catholics, Muslims, Hindus, and others as we united to work for civil rights.

I was a backward country boy raised in the cotton fields and backwoods of Alabama by a family of simple, hardworking, and deeply religious sharecroppers. Diane Nash, another

leader in the student wing of the movement, was a sophisticated city girl from an educated family in Chicago who was
raised Catholic. Bernard Lafayette was a prized son of a Baptist preacher who grew up in Tampa and Philadelphia. And
we were all inspired by the Reverend Kelly Miller Smith, the
well-respected, highly educated pastor of the First Colored
Baptist Church in Nashville, president of the local NAACP,
and ultimately an assistant dean of divinity at Vanderbilt University. Bob Zellner, who did not join the movement until after the events in Nashville, was the defiant son of a Methodist
minister who was also a member of the Ku Klux Klan. Despite vastly different experiences, a common faith connected us
all. It was not exactly the same, but dynamically similar.

This commonality infused the early days of the movement
so that in Nashville particularly, and later within the Student Nonviolent Coordinating Committee (SNCC), we called
ourselves a circle of trust, a band of brothers and sisters
wrapped in the unwavering knowledge that nonviolence had
the power to create change. We not only had grown together
as we discovered the transformative power of nonviolent resistance, but we had risked our lives to see its truth manifested
before our very eyes. We had sounded the trumpet of love
and human unity and the walls of separation came tum-
bling down in Montgomery and in Nashville. This sealed

our confidence in what we believed, and in the early days our faith was unshakable.

As we participated in protest after protest, sit-in after sit-in, where crowds of uncontrollable angry people swarmed around us yelling and jeering, where we were beaten with billy clubs, lead pipes, trampled by horses, and attacked by dogs, our faith was not dampened, as many people today, looking back on the history, often wonder. It actually grew in power and strength. We felt that society had done its worst to us. It had beaten us, arrested us, and put us in jail, and it still could not silence the burning fire for freedom that was guiding our work. Our numbers did not decrease because of an ugly opposition, they increased. Public support for our work did not decrease because of mob violence and police brutality, it increased. It almost seemed the more the unjust resisted, the more impassioned the call for change. After the initial fear, each protest became an exercise in freedom instead of a cause for alarm.

Think about your greatest fear. Consider how you would feel if your life required you to face what you fear the most every day. Ultimately, if you survived the test, you would discover that what you feared actually had no power over you, no power to harm you at all. The freedom you would feel would be so beautiful, so uplifting, so invigorating. People ask me, "How could you be arrested forty times in the movement and never press charges, never fight or strike back?" When people ask these questions, they perceive that I was being abused, when in reality, I was being freed. By the time I stood on the Edmund Pettus Bridge in Selma, I had no fear of physical harm or death. So when people ask me how I managed my fear in that moment, I can truthfully say I was not afraid. I knew by that time that no one had the power to injure me. I had taken that power away by experiencing the worst they could do and discovering it did not diminish me; it did not harm me; it set me free and moved my soul beyond the fear of death.

"I don't know what will happen now . . . But it doesn't really matter with me now. Because I've been to the mountaintop. . . . Like anybody, I would like to live a long life. Longevity has its place. But I am not concerned about that now. I just want to do God's will. And He's allowed me to go up to the mountain. And I've looked over. And I've seen the Promised Land."
—Dr. Martin Luther King Jr.

I think one of the greatest tests of our faith in the movement was being imprisoned in a maximum security facility in the Mississippi Delta, Parchman Farm. It challenged our faith, but it also unlocked our ability to engage in some of the most difficult, yet powerful work of the Civil Rights Movement.

Parchman was, and still is, one of the most brutal prisons in the country. It is a twenty-thousand-acre farm where convicts are subjected to a system of hard labor, and sometimes leased out to farmers to help pick their crops. In other cities, we were incarcerated in jails that were located within the surrounding communities. Parchman was isolated deep in the Yazoo Delta, a remote part of an unyielding state. Contrary to the attempts at revisionist Civil Rights history being propagated today in politics, Mississippi was the most unapologetic, dangerous place to desegregate. Political party affiliation had nothing to do with the jeopardy in which we found ourselves in Mississippi. It was all segregated, all brutally racist, and extremely perilous.

By this point in the Rides, we had already been attacked in Rock Hill, South Carolina, a bus was set on fire in Anniston, Alabama, we had faced mob violence in Birmingham, and spent an entire night in a church in Montgomery surrounded by a bloodthirsty gang of three thousand vigilantes threatening to burn the church down. In Parchman, the National Guard could not come to our aid as it did in Montgomery. We were locked up, locked in, under the control of the state of Mississippi where prisoners had been lynched and murdered with no witnesses, and no traces of their demise. We had no idea what would happen to us when we were arrested and taken to Parchman Farm. We did have a plan, however. Our strategy was that we would not post bail. We would stay incarcerated the entire forty-day term. At the same time, more Freedom Riders would attempt to ride through Mississippi. Knowing they would be arrested, our strategy was to flood the penal system until it overflowed with Americans calling for justice. Just like protestors recently swarmed the state capitol in Wisconsin, we filled the jails in the heart of Mississippi, insisting that our incarceration was wrong.

In the section where I was held, it was very hard to hear and impossible to see the other inmates, but it became clear that our strategy was working. Soon, the cells all around me were full of riders, and we began to sing songs of freedom to remind us of our purpose and keep our spirits high. We sang: "Keep your eyes on the prize, hold on," and "This little light of mine, I'm going to let it shine." We sang "Woke up this morning with my mind stayed on freedom," and many other songs that reminded us of our faith. The songs seemed to aggravate prison officials who ultimately took away our Bibles, our toothbrushes, and even our mattresses and bedding, leaving us to sleep on steel cots, all to snuff out the joy in our hearts. Parchman was a prison meant to break the hardest men, and the prison guards were frustrated that their worst punishment could not shake our faith. We remained incarcerated for a little over a month. We were never let out of our cells in any common area and were only allowed to take a shower once a week. Ultimately, we were released. I guess the state decided punishing us further was counterproductive.

When we were set free from the worst prison in the country, we emerged stronger than ever before. Our faith had seen us through. We knew then that even though Mississippi presented the most perilous dangers in our struggle, we realized through our imprisonment in Parchman that our faith had the power to deliver us even from the most vicious proponents of segregation. That experience set the stage within us spiritually and psychologically to believe that we could open a SNCC office in Greenville, Mississippi, the most resistant territory in the struggle against segregation. It gave us the courage to initiate the Mississippi Freedom Summer, preparing ourselves in advance for the real possibilities of tragedy, and it enabled us to take on the heroic work of the Mississippi Freedom Democratic Party. We came out of Parchman stronger in our faith than ever before, more focused, with a greater sense of purpose. We were like Jonah who had journeyed into the belly of the beast, like Apollo who slayed Python the dragon, like Toussaint L'Ouverture who faced down the most brutal foe. We emerged from Parchman believing we had the power to turn even Mississippi around.

There is still a great deal of work to do today in the Yazoo Delta and the state of Mississippi, but because of a band of brothers and sisters empowered by their faith, the hands that picked cotton in Mississippi are now picking presidents of the United States. Despite the remaining vestiges of segregation, evidently our faith did move mountains because Mississippi has more elected representatives of African American descent today than any other state in the union.

The power of faith is transformative. It can be utilized in your own personal life to change your individual condition, and it can be used as a lifeline of spiritual strength to change a nation. Each and every one of us is imbued with a divine spark of the Creator. That spark links us to the greatest source of power in the universe. It also unites us with one another and the infinity of the Creation. If we stand on this knowledge, even if it is in direct conflict with the greatest forces of injustice around us, a host of divine help, both seen and unseen, will come to our aid. This does not mean you will not face adversity. You can be arrested, jailed, and beaten on this quest, and sometimes you must be prepared to lose all you have, even your life. But if you do not waver, your sacrifice even in death has the power to redeem a community, a people, and a nation from the untruths of separation and division and from the lies of inferiority and superiority. Once you realize your own true divinity, no one can imprison you, reject you, abuse you, or degrade you, and any attempt to do so will only be an aid to your own liberation.

You will discover that no government, no teacher, no abusive parent or spouse, not even torture or terror has the power to define you. Once you find within you the true ability to define yourself according to the dictates of your conscience and your faith, you have come a long way down the path that can lead to social transformation. Faith will be the lifeblood of all your activism, and it has the power to make a way out of no way. You may be in your darkest hour, it may be darker than ten thousand nights on your path to lasting change, but there is something in you that keeps you moving, feeling your way through the night until you can see a glimmer of light. That is the power of faith.

When you pray, move your feet.
—AFRICAN PROVERB

PATIENCE

"Without patience, we will learn less in life. We will see less. We will feel less. We will hear less. Ironically, rush and more usually mean less."
—MOTHER TERESA

The value of restraint, under the right circumstances, can be so profound. Consider the ease, the economy, the wisdom that can accompany the simple act of waiting. Contrary to popular thought, waiting can involve more than defeatist, wishful thinking—it can actually be a pragmatic and realistic catalyst for change. Why? Because it takes our limitations into account. Waiting acknowledges that we are not prime movers in all things. It concedes that there are some factors that lie beyond our control, and any well-considered plan must find a way to manage the unmanageable, to somehow measure and account for the unforeseeable and the unknown, including the work of social change.

The Fifteenth Amendment to the U.S. Constitution was

ratified in 1870 permitting black people to vote; however, exercising that right in Alabama during the Civil Rights Movement truly tested our patience. Although the law had been passed, that right was continually ignored in the Deep South, superseded by a treacherous system of legalized discrimination that dated from the end of the Civil War, exactly one hundred years prior. In the 1960s, Alabama Governor George Wallace was a notoriously outspoken enemy of African American voting rights. His administration held the key to voter registration in Selma, the city that became a reluctant symbol of American racism. The state and county government, law enforcement officials, the White Citizens Council, and the Ku Klux Klan were all determined to keep us from casting our ballots.

During the voting rights struggle, we toiled for years in the vineyard of humanity to create change. We knocked on doors. We held meetings large and small. We organized the unorganized. We constantly trained participants in the philosophy and discipline of nonviolence. We called mass meetings. We sang, prayed, and preached. We protested and strategized ways to demonstrate our plight to audiences in America and around the world. We sacrificed, lived simple lives, and forsook our families and childhood friends. Some of us even abandoned our studies to participate. We had to take action continuously over a period of several years to even begin to make a small dent in such a recalcitrant state, and at the end of every effort we were made to wait.

Some states used what was called a "grandfather clause" to retard our progress after the Fifteenth Amendment passed: Anyone whose grandfather had the right to vote before the Civil War could continue to exercise that right without any impediment. But if a person's grandfather had not been eligible before the war, then he or she had to take a so-called "literacy test" in order to qualify to register to vote in federal elections. Obviously, none of our grandfathers fell into the first category so we had to be prepared to take that test.

To register in Alabama, a person had to fill out a four-page application that was developed by the White Citizens Council, a coalition of businessmen, government officials, and prominent citizens who collectively imposed economic sanctions against any black person who even attempted to register; they could be fired from their jobs, evicted from their homes, foreclosed upon by banks or other lenders. The council made it easy to discover who these folks were. Since the registrar's office was open only during business hours on the first and third Monday of each month, they had to ask for time off from work. In a small rural town, news travels fast. In addition, the names of all applicants were published in the newspaper. As if these methods of intimidation were not discouraging enough, the council would also leak information to the Ku Klux Klan, which was prepared to injure, maim, and kill any African American attempting to vote, threatening families and damaging property to ensure the registrant did not try it again.

The literacy test itself generally comprised three parts. The test varied from any one of one hundred different versions that the registrar could use and administer at will. The first section often required an individual to write out a long, technical passage of the Constitution either by copying the text or taking dictation from the registrar. Most black people were made to take dictation. The registrar noted any errors the applicant made in reproducing the text. The second portion of the test might question the individual on the meaning of the section he or she had been required to duplicate, or it might require him or her to interpret a complicated portion of the Constitution. The last section of the test was a quiz on matters of county and state law.

Once the test was completed, a panel of judges convened in secret to evaluate the responses and determine whether the individual had passed the test. The judges had no responsibility to form their decision based on the answers given on the test and their ruling could not be appealed or reversed. That test was so difficult that college professors, trained lawyers, and teachers were regularly deemed insufficient to pass the test. Recently, I met with Harvard professor Henry Louis Gates. He told me that he read questions from the Alabama literacy test to see whether a Havard professor could pass it. His friend could answer only one out of the three questions he was asked. The test was nearly impossible to pass. In some places officials even threw in a completely irrational measure to further frustrate potential black voters. They might require citizens to count the number of jelly beans in a jar or the number of bubbles in a jar of soap. These kinds of blatant attempts to stop black voter participation were humiliating and demeaning, and, unfortunately, they were effective. In Dallas County, where Selma is the county seat, there were fifteen thousand eligible African American voters; by early 1965 only three hundred of them were registered to vote.

The Student Nonviolent Coordinating Committee, the organization I chaired, began organizing people, developing Citizenship Schools to educate residents about the power of the vote and the importance of voter registration. We also taught them skills that would help them pass the literacy test. We told them how casting a ballot could impact the future of their schools, roads, housing opportunities, treatment by law enforcement, job opportunities, business development, water and electricity supplies, and so much more. We held mass meetings at Brown Chapel AME Church to pass out information and encourage people's spirits. We trained them in the tactics of nonviolence, and prepared them psychologically for the difficulties that lay ahead: harassment, threats, possible beating, arrest, imprisonment, and even death. Having grown up in Selma, they knew what was at stake even better than many SNCC volunteers.

All of these tactics were necessary to achieve our goal. To be certain, we took action and employed every method we knew to attack the problem. However, the ultimate battleground in this conflict was not in a classroom or standing in line on a city sidewalk. It was behind the door of the registrar's office. Despite all our organization and action, the key to our access to the ballot box was in someone else's hands. We had to be granted entrance to the registrar's office, and the registrar made sure the office was closed more than it was open. Even on the off chance that we got in, we had to labor through a long examination and await the decision of an unjust panel who almost always denied us, regardless of our competency. We had to wait for the registrar to open the office. We had to wait to be granted entrance, wait to prepare for the test, wait to take the test, await the results, and wait for an unjust system to change.

Though in these matters our only option was to wait, we

never regarded this as a passive position. We perceived that waiting could be viewed as an elegant way to prove a point, and we used it as a tool to demonstrate the inaccessibility of the vote in Alabama. We staged large demonstrations on the days it was possible to register to vote in Selma, and toward the end of the struggle, especially when Martin Luther King Jr. got involved, we protested on other days as well. Hundreds of citizens from Selma and the surrounding communities gathered in the morning and simply stood in line the entire day in a peaceful and orderly fashion. We waited in the sweltering summer sun, under the cooling clouds of moody winter days, and in the humid rain of spring. We stood in lines that never moved, carrying signs, singing freedom songs on the green marble courthouse steps, patiently hoping the registrar would open the door and allow us to enter. We waited day in and day out for two years. The courthouse was not far from the police station, and Sheriff Jim Clark and his men were on constant watch. Although we waited patiently and in peace, our persistence was considered an act of aggression by the sheriff, and he used this as an excuse to condone violence. Hundreds of us were arrested, and some were beaten and taken to jail.

We reduced the danger of brutality by ensuring that the national media were well informed of our intentions. On some occasions, they joined us as observers, keeping a watchful eye, not realizing they were indirectly protecting us from the potential of greater physical abuse. We knew that no matter how vicious Southerners could be in the dark, they would not want to see themselves in the light portrayed as violent racists to a nation of television viewers and newspaper and magazine readers.

We could have stormed the clerk's office or demanded entrance, but that would have been a violation of every principle we were trying to uphold. It would have been an illogical invitation to violence, and we had no capacity to match the guns, nightsticks, dogs, and mounted forces of the Alabama state troopers. Many of us would have been killed while others were landing in jail, never to walk free again, and the credibility of our cause would have been severely damaged. Any aggressive demand for immediate results would have failed miserably. Our desire was not to register at any cost, if the price was sacrificing our dignity and self-respect. It is important to understand that we weren't in the business of destruction. We wanted to build and not tear down, to unify and not divide, to love and not plant the seeds of hate.

We never raised our fists. All we did was wait, but that waiting acted like a ramrod that broke down the doors of resistance. It reflected poorly on Sheriff Clark and his men.

We were very aware that our civility demonstrated above all the absurdity of brutalizing peaceful, law-abiding citizens and detaining them from exercising their constitutional rights. One day, Sheriff Clark called me an "outside agitator" and "the lowest form of humanity." I told him, "Sheriff, I may be an agitator but I am not an outsider. I grew up only forty miles from here, and these people are going to stay here until we are allowed to register to vote." I was arrested and taken to jail, along with hundreds of others, for simply telling the truth.

Ultimately, our strategy worked. After years of waiting, we exposed the injustice of our opposition. The voting rights struggle in Alabama ended with what some legal scholars have called the most effective piece of legislation the U.S. Congress had passed in over fifty years: the Voting Rights Act of 1965. Previously, President Lyndon Johnson had advised us it would be impossible to pass another bill on the heels of the passage of the Civil Rights Act of 1964, which made discrimination in public accommodations illegal. But because of the people of Selma, Alabama, and the thousands who supported them, because of the people who demonstrated beyond a shadow of a doubt the pressing need for justice, Johnson was able to send a voting rights bill to the floor of the House. When he introduced the bill, he said these unforgettable words, which I often repeat in my speeches today: "At times history and fate meet at a single time in a single place to shape a turning point in man's unending search for freedom. So it was at Lexington and Concord. So it was a century ago at Appomattox. So it was last week in Selma, Alabama."

The people of Selma wrote that act with their marching feet. It was their determination to wait without ceasing that dramatically altered American history. The Voting Rights Act outlawed literacy tests and grandfather clauses, but it also provided for periodic reauthorization to curtail present-day efforts to limit free and fair access to the ballot box. It allowed unfair gerrymandering and voting changes to be monitored and even overruled by the Justice Department. It provided for American citizens who are members of all kinds of language minorities, from Latinos to Vietnamese to Eskimos and Native Americans, to participate in the democratic process.

I should mention here that the Voting Rights Act is under attack today. A series of court cases has been mounted in several states, angled toward the Supreme Court with the hope that the most powerful section of the act, section 5, will be nullified. There are still groups working to suppress the vote through the requirement of government-issued photo IDs, to manipulate the Office of the Secretary of State, end weekend or early voting, and infuse dubiously malfunctioning voting machines into the process.

That is why it is very important to remain engaged, especially when it is aggravating. The vote is the most powerful nonviolent tool we have to make change in a democratic society, but one vote will not make all the change that is necessary. Change requires patient, persistent action.

To most of us, patience seems almost too simple. In order to feel effective and in command, we require control that brings immediate results. We have a "fast-food mentality" that expects an instant return on our investment of time, attention, and effort, a return that is concrete and clear. We are so comfortable charging forward and succeeding through our aggression and innovation that the idea of patience can seem contrary to our instincts. Yet, I assure you, as I have seen through my very eyes: even a little patience can pay big dividends.

Today, as a U.S. congressman, I can offer a few insights on how you may encourage the government to take action. Certainly creative nonviolent protests timed to impact legislative actions like important votes or hearings are strategic options. Persistent demonstrations prove there is a demand among the people for change. But a one-day protest or a perfunctory march is not the kind of resounding proof that is needed to clearly define a mobilized constituency. Persistent, dedicated, determined action does. It provides unequivocal leverage for members of Congress who are inclined to vote with you, and it educates and informs members who are on the fence, offering room within the legislative process for persuasive negotiations that lead to more favorable votes on particular issues.

Education might also be one of the most important tools that an organized, determined people need to institute change. People need to be informed about the legislative process and the structure of our government. Ours is a diffuse, complex political system. Its benefit is that no one official or agency has unilateral authority to dictate to the people, so no one entity can enforce its will without experiencing some kind of check from the other branches. For example, the U.S. House of Representatives can pass legislation that will never get through the Senate. The Senate is a check on the House and vice versa. If legislation does pass both bodies, it still must be signed by the president, who has veto power, before it can become law. If an unjust law is still able to pass through this gauntlet, then lawsuits can be filed in court, which can negate the power of that legislation or rule it entirely unconstitutional. This series of "gates and levers" was a wise complication developed by our founders, who themselves had been victimized by tyranny. So viewed another way, it could be perceived that the logjam making people frustrated with government today is not a demonstration that "Washington is broken," as so many pundits like to say, but that this system of checks and balances is working. Without this logjam, there would be forces ramming through legislation that would change the relationship between the people and its government for many years to come.

That is the benefit of a checks-and-balances system, to be sure; however, it is complex. Yet the complexity of this system is both beneficial and burdensome. It is good because it presents a shield against injustice. It is difficult because it can be complex to navigate. But it is that very complexity that has made our government so durable, and having the patience to learn to navigate its intricacies will only serve you well in the long run. We have to recognize that there is no one-stop shop in our system, so seeing the desired results requires information, persistence, and patience.

I have been amazed that so many people are completely unaware of what their U.S. representatives do. My job is to represent the views, problems, and successes of the people of the fifth congressional district of Georgia, which mainly includes the city of Atlanta, throughout the federal decision-making process. I use my influence and seniority to gain the attention of federal legislators and the executive branch so they understand specific problems in my district. I meet with constituents and their representatives who share their concerns with me to ensure I gather support and resources to help address their needs. And I vote on federal legislation to protect their interests and manage their concerns.

If I determine that problems within my district reflect a national trend, I work on creating a bill that helps all jurisdictions facing the same problem. For example, if I note veterans are overrepresented in the homeless population in my district and that this problem persists in communities nationwide, I work with members of Congress who sit on pertinent committees such as the Veterans Affairs Committee and the Appropriations Committee. Together we may develop legislation to authorize a unit, for example, that tracks and treats homeless veterans living on the streets in any city.

Solving the problem of homelessness is a multifaceted problem, however. There is no quick fix. The federal government cannot implement all the solutions itself, because it does not have sole jurisdiction over all the areas of public life that the problem affects. It may require a partnership between the government, private and nonprofit organizations, churches, shelters, health services, community groups, citizen volunteers, job placement organizations, housing programs, banks, and training facilities. For instance, the city may offer funding to nonprofits to develop a food program or ask for donations from local restaurants and grocery stores to help resolve the hunger that is part of homelessness, while public health agencies may help the sick get treatment and medications. The state may create a fund for combating homelessness in its major cities, and request its U.S. representative or senator to secure federal monies to support these programs. It might also enlist the aid of congressional representatives in applying for grants from federal agencies.

All of these solutions are subject to the politics of the time. If the federal budget is in a deficit, as it is now, the federal program offering funding for the homeless might not receive any appropriations in that budgeting cycle. This would require the state and its congressional representatives to start over and try to get funding again in the next budget.

Meanwhile, what do citizens see? They see homeless people on the street as they had before, and they may assume that their elected representatives do not care and nothing has been done. As you can see, many factors impact every stage of the process. If effective tactics are employed at strategic moments, just before a vote or when a measure is up for debate, they can boldly underline the people's will in the matter, which goes a long way toward convincing elected representatives to act.

Passage of a bill can be circuitous, especially if it is controversial or has an adverse effect on a large American constituency. Trying to pass the kind of bill I suggested above in a legislative environment where Congress is cutting services and entitlements would be almost impossible, but that does not mean the idea is not worthwhile, or that it will never pass. Be persistent and consistent in your activism and, most important, be patient. If you continue to advocate for what you believe is right, there may come a time when people will change their thinking, and once they are looking for a good legislative idea, your work will be at the forefront of their minds.

Informed activism requires reading the newspaper, tracking bills through the Library of Congress's THOMAS website, and watching legislative debates on C-SPAN. It also means learning which legislators on all levels sit on committees that affect your issue. Build relationships with these people because they can keep you apprised of legislative action and, once you persuade them to come over to your side, they are the ones who will be drafting the legislation that reflects your point of view.

Even as a member of Congress, ideas that I believe in may take years, even decades, to be signed into law. One of the highlights of my congressional career was the final authorization and mandate to build the National Museum of African American History and Culture on the National Mall in Washington. Yet, seeing this project come to fruition tested the patience and perseverance of many generations.

In 1915, an organization of black Civil War veterans who

had been repeatedly snubbed in Washington, at a time when other veterans of the war were celebrated by the nation, decided to form the National Museum Association. Its goal was to erect a beautiful cultural archive honoring the history and contributions of African Americans to this country.

By 1919, the association had convinced almost every governor in the country to appoint a representative to sit on the advisory board of this committee, and Congress was seriously considering legislation to authorize building the new memorial. A grassroots movement had grown in support of the museum, and rallies had been mounted in several cities with thousands in attendance.

In 1920, the House Committee on the Library requested the Commission on Fine Arts to implement plans to build a National Mall. An internal memo was generated suggesting several areas on this mall as a possible location for the new museum. However, the memo was never sent to Congress. Instead, the commission recommended that a Negro memorial should be deferred until after a monument was built to the veterans of World War I.

Members of the National Museum Association persisted. For fourteen years they worked, getting several bills passed through Congress to authorize construction, but they still faced significant obstacles. At that time lynching was rampant, especially throughout the South. Antilynching activists like Colonel Charles Young, the third African American to graduate from West Point, felt the most important memorial to the fallen black soldier would be legislation that ended lynching and legal discrimination. Some felt African Americans did not deserve a national museum, others thought it was too costly, another group believed the project should stand in line behind a memorial dedicated to Thomas Jefferson, and still others thought honoring the role of black mammies was more appropriate.

Finally, in March of 1929, President Calvin Coolidge signed a law authorizing this national museum. However, the museum bill had encountered such vehement opposition during debate in Congress that all funding for it had been depleted. The black newspapers ridiculed the legislation calling it a joke. The lack of funding required all necessary resources to be raised from private interests.

To add insult to injury, five months later, the stock market crashed, dashing any hope of raising enough private equity to back the project. The Great Depression ensued, and in December of 1929, the committee appointed to move this project along met with President Hoover to request $1.6 million in Reconstruction-era funds. Though Secretary of the Treasury Andrew Mellon verified the funds were indeed available, neither Hoover nor Congress acted on the request. Four years later, President Franklin Roosevelt disbanded the committee altogether.

About thirty-four years went by, and plans to build a museum honoring Afro American history resurged after the death of Martin Luther King Jr. Several bills were introduced in the House and Senate to study the possibility of a national museum. At the same time, Rep. Clarence Brown and Sen. John Glenn, both members of the Ohio delegation, introduced legislation to establish a national museum of Negro history and culture in Wilberforce, Ohio, to be run by the National Park Service. The idea was opposed by the Interior Department, which did not believe a national museum should be located outside of Washington, D.C. The Smithsonian Institution agreed with the Interior Department's criticism in principle, but it did not support a separate museum set aside to commemorate the African American contribution. Its position was that it already incorporated that history into its other museums.

In 1980, Congress again appointed a committee to study the issue, charging it to report back in two years. Congress once again appropriated no operating funds to carry out this study. Finally, five years later, Sen. Glenn was able to win a small appropriation of $200,000 for the committee. But by this time, the committee's focus had turned away from the Wilberforce site to a building on the National Mall. Enter Mickey Leland, a young, intelligent representative from Texas, elected because of the effectiveness of the Voting Rights Act. Under his leadership in 1985, Congress passed a joint resolution to support the committee's effort to privately endow the building of a museum to commemorate African American history and culture, managed by the National Park Service. This effort waned as more support gathered for building a museum on the National Mall.

I was elected to Congress in 1986, and in 1988 I joined Leland and Sen. Paul Simon of Illinois to introduce bills in the House and Senate to create a National African American Heritage Memorial Museum within the Smithsonian Institution. The next year, Leland, a member of the Select Committee on World Hunger who had pushed through an $800 million aid package to help sub-Saharan African drought victims, was killed in a tragic plane crash while on a trip to investigate the famine in Ethiopia.

I then took up the charge to win passage of the museum bill. Our 1989 bill specified placement on the National Mall and mandated a building that was at least 377,000 square feet. Hearings were held on the museum in August of that year after Leland's plane crash, but still no go. The Smithsonian, however, headed by Robert McCormick, did appoint a blue-ribbon commission to study the development of this museum, including Smithsonian curators and directors such as Bernice Johnson Reagon, a curator for the Museum of American History who had been a member of SNCC; Spencer Crew, another Smithsonian curator; Lerone Bennett, executive editor of *Ebony*; the fine artist David Driskell; scholar Cornel West of Princeton University; A. B. Spelman of the National Endowment for the Arts; and Deborah Willis, head of the photographs division of the Schomberg Center for Research in Black Culture in New York.

The committee ultimately determined that a national museum was warranted, that it should be managed by the Smithsonian Institution, and deemed it should be housed in a one-hundred-year-old part of the historic Smithsonian called the Arts and Industries building. The greatest controversy surrounding the report was the idea to place the museum in an aging building. Rep. Gus Savage of Illinois was the most vocal critic, and during the 1992 hearings he demanded to know why the museum could not be newly built on the National Mall as others had been. Two years later, Savage was no longer a member of Congress and the House passed a bill authorizing the museum in the Arts and Industries building. However, passage was blocked by Sen. Jesse Helms of North Carolina.

In the meantime, regardless of all these setbacks, in every session of Congress I persisted in introducing the legislation. I did this for over a decade with no results, still undaunted in my belief that this was the right thing to do, and on my watch I was determined to do my part to make it happen. We saw many new museums built on the mall: the African Art Museum, the Air and Space Museum, the Museum of the American Indian, and many more in this time. I hired a very enterprising legislative director, Tammy Boyd, who began working on every angle to get the bill through. Finally, in 2001, I introduced a bill authorizing the National Museum of African American History and Culture, in conjunction with Rep. J. C. Watts of Oklahoma on the House side. Sens. Max Cleland of Georgia and Sam Brownback of Kansas agreed to introduce the same bill on the Senate side. The bill provided $15 million for planning and operations and $10 million for educational programs. The bill was finally passed by Congress. A presidential commission was formed to study the contentious issues regarding site placement. I had introduced the same bill in Congress for fifteen years; Rep. Leland had done his part in the years before me; and the entire effort had begun eighty-eight years before. But the bill was finally signed into law in 2003. The National Museum of African American History and Culture will be built on the National Mall, scheduled to be completed in 2015, a full 100 years after the idea was first conceived.

Patience is a guiding light in all the work of change. It is an aspect of the commitment people make to finish what they start. Once you have begun the work involved in creating change, moving an idea forward step-by-step, doing all that is within your power, and understanding that there will be forces beyond your control that may support you or block you is central to the change you seek. There is a process to everything. You must follow certain steps, and each one of those steps must be patiently, persistently, and thoroughly implemented to receive the best outcome. Even setbacks can serve a vital purpose to completing your goal.

Take a long, hard look down the road you will have to travel once you have made a commitment to work for change. Know that this transformation will not happen right away. Change often takes time. It rarely happens all at once. In the movement, we didn't know how history would play itself out. When we were getting arrested and waiting in jail or standing in unmovable lines on the courthouse steps, we didn't know what would happen, but we knew it had to happen.

Use the words of the movement to pace yourself. We used to say that ours is not the struggle of one day, one week, or one year. Ours is not the struggle of one judicial appointment or presidential term. Ours is the struggle of a lifetime, or maybe even many lifetimes, and each one of us in every generation must do our part. And if we believe in the change we seek, then it is easy to commit to doing all we can, because the responsibility is ours alone to build a better society and a more peaceful world.

STUDY

"Our deepest fear is not that we are inadequate.
Our deepest fear is that we are powerful beyond measure. It is our
light, not our darkness that most frightens us. We ask ourselves,
'Who am I to be brilliant, gorgeous, talented and fabulous?'
Actually, who are you not to be? You are a child of God.
Your playing small doesn't serve the world. There is nothing
enlightened about shrinking so that other people won't feel
insecure around you. We were born to make manifest the glory of
God that is within us. It is not just in some of us; it's in everyone.
And when we let our own light shine, we unconsciously give other
people permission to do the same. As we are liberated from our
own fear, our presence automatically liberates others."

—MARIANNE WILLIAMSON

Many people believe that because we focused on breaking unjust laws and evil traditions, that our movement was free-form, spontaneous, and unrehearsed. Nothing could be further from the truth. We did not just wake up one day and decide to march on Washington or from Selma to Montgomery. We studied, we strategized, we organized, trained, and prepared to take action. Most of what we accomplished grew out of years, decades, and even centuries of groundwork that was laid before most of us were even born, and those at the center of the struggle studied that history and used its wisdom to develop the strategic actions of the movement. From the legacy left by past generations, we gained a significant understanding of how we should forge ahead.

It is only through examining history that you become aware of where you stand within the continuum of change. You may find you are the "voice crying in the wilderness" who will have to walk alone. Or you may find only a few devotees who will join you throughout the whole period of your activism. This does not mean your work is not important. It means the part you must play is simply different than those leaders who stand at the front lines of a mass movement. Every contribution is important to the work of change, and it is only when you study the history of activism that you can perceive what your role may be and how others managed in the same kind of position years and decades before. It is through study and preparation that you can increase the power of your work.

I meet so many ambitious young politicians and leaders who want to jump to the head of the line. They do not know how we arrived at this point in our history as a nation, but they believe they should be appointed to lead us into the future. They think that because they are educated, articulate, and talented someone should usher them down the red carpet to a throne of leadership. But real leaders are not appointed. They emerge out of the masses of the people and rise to the forefront through the circumstances of their lives. Either their inner journey or their human experience prepares them to take that role. They do not nominate themselves. They are called into service by a spirit moving through a people that points to them as the embodiment of the cause they serve.

Growing up, my family and community were loving and accepting, but the world around us was full of so much hate. There was no NAACP chapter in my community—the organization had been banned in Alabama—so there was no activist community I could engage with to validate my deep sense of frustration and agitation. Most of the people around me, including my parents, did not believe it was constructive to complain about the unfairness of our way of life. They knew it was not right, but they could not see a way to change it. I could not figure a way out either, especially as a child, but in the center of my being I never stopped looking for one.

I was lucky to be born at a peak of activism, just as the wave of change was about to crest in the United States, when gifted leaders like Martin Luther King Jr., Jim Lawson, and A. Philip Randolph were all alive and engaged in the same movement. Many of us in the movement were young and impatient, but we studied and prepared ourselves to confront the challenges of our time, and we respected the elder activists whose work charted the path to our future. Some of this was conscious preparation and other aspects seemed to involve a kind of divine orchestration that ordered our steps and brought people together from unlikely places to play a role in history. It is important for upcoming activists to study American history, as well as political and philosophical thought. It is unlikely that what you hope to accomplish is new. Current activism is almost always linked to the history of revolution worldwide, and Americans have a special connection to this legacy because our nation was born out of the struggle against tyranny.

So if we study the story of the Civil Rights Movement, we see that it was not by accident that someone like Martin Luther King Jr. became a great minister at the head of a movement. His is the quintessential example of leadership in the twentieth century, in my estimation, so it is important to study how he came to lead. He was born with a gift and placed within a set of circumstances that shaped and polished his talent. But King did not solely rely on what was bestowed on him. He made a conscious effort to build his merit through academic pursuits. He dressed well. He was articulate and well spoken, but that was not his focus. Those attributes were incidental to his emergence at the forefront of history. His primary concern was always on the substance of injustice. The people of Montgomery, the place where he began his career as the pastor, needed more than polish and shine. They needed someone with a deep understanding of the problems that met them at every turn. It was King's commitment to search for answers to the problems of his people that made him fit for leadership, and it was his heritage that prepared him for it.

King was born into the bosom of leadership within a family of prominent ministers, and he lived in the city that would become the headquarters for the struggle for civil rights. When he became co-pastor of Ebenezer Baptist Church in 1960, King was carrying on a legacy, becoming the third generation to helm the church, preceded by his father and maternal grandfather.

As Martin Luther King Jr. evaluated the ministers he knew, he noticed that many lacked sophistication and a depth of religious training and academic knowledge, so he determined to enter the field with the best training he could attain. He wanted to distinguish himself and take ministry to a more professional level, not simply become a part of the crowd. He was also an intelligent and curious child who faced the cruel disappointments of racism with an inquiring mind. Most people who are raised under the oppression of social discrimination can recall the exact moment when they realized others saw them as different. King's realization was not unusual. It happened to him as it did for many children: when he turned school-age. As a toddler he was fast friends with a little white boy, who played near his father's store in King's neighborhood. But once the boys became school-age, they were sent to separate schools, and King noticed the boy suddenly stopped coming to play. King was heartbroken. He simply could not understand why his friend didn't visit him anymore. When he asked his parents about his disappointment, they revealed to him the system of discrimination and segregation that surrounded him. Years later, as a young high school student, the irony of winning an oratorical contest wasn't lost on King either. Although his award-winning speech was about the paradox of discrimination in a nation where freedom was protected by law and revered in the words of its founding Constitution, on the bus trip back from the contest he and his teacher were made to get up from their seats and stand for fifty miles after some white passengers boarded the bus.

King was aggravated by these problems, but not daunted. The intellectual environment surrounding him and the numerous discussions he had overheard and engaged in with his parents and their friends who were scholars, ministers, and businessmen in the Atlanta community gave him a context to wrestle with these issues mentally. He was determined to understand how a religion that commanded him to love could resolve the problems of a people surrounded by hate. He held this question in his mind throughout his entire academic experience and saw his scholarship as an opportunity to search for an answer.

He graduated from Morehouse at nineteen, and by the time he was twenty-three years old he held a doctorate in divinity from Boston College and a degree in divinity from Crozer Theological Seminary. He never forgot his purpose or his people in his work, and he used the mandates of graduate research to begin developing his own brand of social gospel. In his quest, he made it a point to study the work of all the major theologians and philosophers who might have had any bearing on his thesis. He also branched out beyond his comfort zone, as any credible scholar would, to study influential ideas of the time that were antithetical to his beliefs, like the work of Marx, Lenin, and Nietzsche. He examined every possible angle to find the theological answers to the questions he was asking, and he emerged in his study as a notable student and a compelling scholar.

One day he heard that Mordecai Johnson, the esteemed president of Howard University and also a minister, Morehouse graduate, and a gifted public speaker, was lecturing in Philadelphia. King decided to travel from Boston to hear Johnson speak. It was there that he heard the name Mohandas Gandhi for the first time. King was electrified by Johnson's discussion of the nonviolent revolution in India, and when he returned from the outing he read everything he could find on Gandhi. His testament and philosophy were the critical missing links that helped King formulate an American strategy for overcoming segregation. Once he discovered these ideas he could have taught them in the protection of an ivory tower of a university. He certainly had enough offers to stay in the North and inspire the intellectual achievements of his students. But given the choice, he decided to return to the South to avail himself of the opportunity to participate in the struggle and put these notions to the test. He was aware that he was choosing between security and the likelihood that struggle would mean trouble, but he felt the imperative to practice what he would preach. So when the people of Montgomery called him to the forefront to serve as the leader of the boycott, he had done his share of studying, had reflected on an American approach to protest steeped in a deep legacy and theology that crossed the boundaries of nations and faiths, even at the young age of twenty-six.

IT TOOK TWENTY-THREE years for King to prepare himself to be the kind of outstanding minister that others have spent a lifetime trying to emulate. His command in the profession was rooted in more than just training; there was also a deep respect for the legacy that preceded him. He did not discard that heritage as the wisdom of another age, but he drew upon that history of his faith and the proven philosophies of protest to build his understanding. Yet his respect for the past did not offer King satisfaction with the status quo. He added to his profession by reaching for new experiences, taking advantage of educational opportunities outside the comfort zone of what he knew and had witnessed in Atlanta. In King we see the virtue of patience at work. He took his time and did his research as he evolved into the man he wanted to become. He also had faith in the hand of the divine to use him and all he had garnered at the appropriate time and place. He never clamored to be rich, famous, the best dressed, or the most articulate. But he had a vision of how he wanted to serve and he moved toward that vision. He studied, prepared, and readied himself so that he was the most able servant available.

THE STORY OF King's road to leadership reflects the power of study to prepare the mind to command a people and leave a lasting legacy. The refinements of his academic preparation tend to overshadow the role that the spirit played in his ascent to becoming a civil rights icon, even though there is no question that King could never have become the symbol of a non-violent revolution without a calling from the spirit. That is what gave him the power to minister to a people and a nation.

SOME PEOPLE ARE tracked down by what I call the spirit of history, to play a role in the evolution of humankind. My experience stands as a striking contrast to King's very steady, visible path to leadership. In my case, it's hard to draw a straight line that defines exactly how I came to lead. My story shows how the spirit can order a person's steps. It can pluck him or her from the most unlikely place to stand on the front lines of change.

As a child, I grew up around people others may have viewed as poor or impoverished, but these people were actually rich: rich in character and rich in faith. They may have been denied the most basic material resources, but they did not lack the drive. No matter what life affords you in material goods you can rise above any circumstances through your adherence to high standards and a commitment to following the lead of your own spirit. Having values and holding on to our beliefs is what got us through and it's what will get you through. I never felt I was the underdog. I never felt that I was poor or deprived. I discovered after I left my parents' farm that other people viewed me as country or poor, but it was never how I saw myself. And it was never due to any self-defeating notion my parents or my community passed on to me. My upbringing, my community, my faith gave me confidence because it was not based on an external definition of our value. We knew we were children of the divine, so we believed in our own worth, regardless what the world might say.

I went to school, but unlike King I could only go sporadically because there were times the fields had to be planted or harvested. The only money the local government contributed to the schooling of black children in Alabama was the teacher's salary. A financially strapped black community had to pay for everything else. We used old, hand-me-down textbooks the whites no longer needed, and just one teacher was responsible for educating students in several different grades.

When I was fifteen years old, the bus boycott was unfolding in Montgomery forty miles away from my home. Our family could not afford a newspaper subscription, but my grandfather had one, so I would read his paper, hungry for information. I was anxious to learn about any action taken to defend our dignity. And then one day, on an old radio, I heard the voice of Martin Luther King Jr. I could tell he was a young man from the South, just like me. He was preaching about the responsibility of Christians to respond to the injustices of segregation. He was delivering the message I had prayed to hear. He was answering the gnawing questions in my soul struggling to find a way out. King had found a way, and it was consistent with my dream to see the power of love manifest more than anything, to see hate eradicated and wrong made right.

When I heard King it was as though a light turned on in my heart. When I heard his voice, I felt he was talking directly to me. From that moment on, I decided I wanted to be just like him. Immediately, I wrote to New York to join a chapter of the NAACP, since Alabama did not have one, and to this day I am a member of the New York chapter. One day my mother brought home a brochure describing American Baptist Theological Seminary in Nashville (ABT). I wanted to go to King's alma mater, Morehouse, but my grades weren't good enough, and we couldn't afford it. ABT, however, offered an undergraduate program for aspiring ministers that allowed students to work their way through college. I knew immediately that it was the place for me. Little did I know being in Nashville would position me at the heart of nonviolent activism, or that I would have the opportunity to work alongside the man I deeply admired. I couldn't anticipate what the future would hold. At that time I was just following my heart, my desire to do something, and somehow, someway, the Creator ordered my steps and placed me right where I needed to be to play a role in the work for change.

When I arrived in Nashville, people thought I was backward, country, and shy. My resources were few, but my ability to commune with the spirit and allow myself to be guided by it propelled me to the center of change. I did not have the kind of material and intellectual resources that King had. Instead, mine was a kind of inner preparation, a silent communion with a higher power that is still a part of my daily life today. My adherence to the inner voice allowed me to participate in a movement for good. I say this to let you know that preparation can take many different forms. Not everyone is left a family legacy as rich as Martin Luther King Jr.'s, or has the same gifts and privileges, but there is a power that can raise you up even from the lowliest of places and guide you to the forefront of change if you truly want to create a better world.

"It's the action, not the fruit of the action, that's important.
You have to do the right thing. It may not be in your power,
may not be in your time, that there'll be any fruit.
But that doesn't mean you stop doing the right thing.

You may never know what results come from your action.
But if you do nothing, there will be no result."
—MOHANDAS GANDHI

What we accomplished back then is directly connected to many of the advances we see today. The activists of today have no need to "reinvent the wheel." There is a lineage of struggle in America and around the world that can be used as a source of inspiration and instruction by anyone who is seriously interested in confronting the highest levels of power to make change. In my travels to England, India, Germany, South Africa, as well as through reports from Ireland, Japan, and Russia, I have met people involved in their own indigenous struggles who say they study the books and films documenting the Civil Rights Movement intensely, to glean strategy and principles of activism to use in their own societies.

It is no accident that the young people of Egypt could be heard chanting words we began using in protests on the streets in America forty years prior. When I heard the citizens in Tahrir Square shouting, "The people united will never be defeated," it made me feel so good to see the seeds we planted decades ago were blossoming in another form. I was proud that the people of Egypt held to nonviolent principles, regardless of the brutality they faced. Later I read that Dalia Ziada, the Egypt director of the American Islamic Congress (AIC), was responsible for resurrecting a comic book we used extensively in the movement. On the cover was a drawing of Martin Luther King Jr., a Montgomery bus, and the dome of the Alabama state capitol. The AIC did their own research, found the comic book, and had it translated into Arabic to help spread the message and means of nonviolent protest throughout the masses of citizens gathered in Tahrir Square. They distributed two thousand copies of the comic book across Egypt. Fifty years ago, the Fellowship of Reconciliation distributed two hundred and fifty thousand throughout America. I invited Ziada to come to my office, and she gave me a copy of that comic book. She also told me that Egyptian students had received nonviolence training based on the training we received from Jim Lawson and others in the movement, except theirs was managed by Serbian dissidents who had used those tactics to create change in their own society. An international network of student activists had developed worldwide and they were training, teaching, and preparing one another in a way that ultimately became the Arab Spring. And then those seeds were regerminated in America, so that the actions of the people in the Middle East gave the people of Wisconsin courage to occupy the statehouse, and they, in turn, gave courage to those who decided to begin the Occupy movement in the United States. And now we see waves of change shifting and moving across international boundaries, based on a common understanding of how peaceful protest can create change. Study and preparation created this movement.

Each uprising of the people informs and seeds the others, especially in the age of the Internet. In Tunisia, word of an act of righteous indignation—a vendor who set himself on fire to protest the unjust confiscation of his property—spread like wildfire over Facebook and ultimately ended the regime of a tyrant.

During the Civil Rights Movement, we didn't have the Internet. We did not have iPhones or computers. We didn't even have fax machines. We had no power of celebrity, no money. But we had ourselves. So we used what we had. We put our bodies on the line for simple justice and social change. We did all we could, and by the power of grace, it was enough to create transformation. Our poise was not founded on money, breeding, or education, but rather on our spiritual lineage and unbreakable connection to the divine. What we could not muster was added through a grace that never failed, a stream of consciousness that was never interrupted by external circumstance. The spirit adds what we cannot offer to an end result that is more in keeping with the dictates of the universe. Any activist must have faith in this spiritual legacy, that in the work of change, we are not alone, but there are forces that assist us and act in concert with us. I will never forget our march across the Edmund Pettus Bridge, before we met the sea of blue Alabama state troopers on the other side. We walked two by two, totally in faith, not knowing what our end would be. We were silent. Just six hundred of us walking in a quiet persistence. To me, it felt like a holy march, so solemn, so reverent, so filled with unity and purpose. Though in the pictures we look so alone, I felt like there was a band of brothers and sisters, the seen and the unseen who marched with us. Our spirits joined with others through the ages who had determined to stand for justice, and they were also there.

Had it not been for the struggles and sacrifices of the 1950s and '60s, Barack Obama would never have been elected president of the United States. In turn, were we not inspired by the advancements of Mohandas Gandhi in South Africa and India, the organizing tactics developed by the Labor Movement in the early decades of the twentieth century, as well as a commitment to nonviolence sealed in Europe during the first days of World War I, the American history we participated in creating would have been entirely different, and maybe much less influential. Every generation leaves behind a legacy. What that legacy will be is determined by the people of that generation. What legacy do you want to leave behind?

Your generation will have new leaders and will use different methods of struggle, but the purpose will be the same. You will be marching toward the next visionary horizon with the radiance of faith and truth, preparing the way for peace and reconciliation, building a highway that channels the almighty power of love as a guiding force in all the affairs of humankind, and your soul will join with those souls who have struggled for freedom, from the dawn of humanity.

"It is from numberless diverse acts of courage and belief that human history is shaped. Each time a man stands up for an ideal, or acts to improve the lot of others, or strikes out against injustice, he sends forth a tiny ripple of hope, and crossing each other from a million different centers of energy and daring, those ripples build a current that can sweep down the mightiest walls of oppression and resistance."
—ROBERT F. KENNEDY

TRUTH

"The truth is incontrovertible. Malice may attack it, ignorance may deride it, but in the end, there it is."
—WINSTON CHURCHILL

The truth is a powerful force. It is the foundation of all things. The truth is so all consuming that it cannot be denied. You cannot erase the truth. You cannot tarnish the truth. You cannot whitewash the truth. It is bigger than the sum of us all, and whole, even in its parts.

And yet, even though the truth can't be denied or erased, it can be systemically obscured, strategically misinterpreted, and hidden from mainstream comprehension. Our faith in the movement was that we could peel back the falsehood of all our conditioning, scrape away the hard, crusty cynicism of our politics, and peer through to the root of social dysfunction. That journey beyond the limits of normal discourse would lead to the central, simple principles of life, based on the unfathomable, massive bedrock of the truth. In SNCC, a "leaderless" organization, we viewed consensus as a guiding principle. Sometimes we would spend all night, even days as a group discussing the merits of one idea until all the opposition was quieted and all conflict subsided. Ultimately, the dissolution of SNCC, at its core, emanated around different perceptions of the truth.

The quest for the truth was the center of Gandhi's nonviolent activism. Much of his prayer and spiritual practice focused on arriving at an evermore pure understanding of eternal truth, according to his faith. He believed that individual revelation about actions that violate the dignity of any manifestation of life energy—whether human, animal, or biological—conferred a responsibility to act without compromise or regression. That accounts for his stripping away much of the trappings of his life as a lawyer. It is why he took up the simple dress, lifestyle, and occupation of the Indian villager who he believed represented the essence of Indian life.

The search for truth must be a vital part of any activist's life or that of any movement because it conveys meaning to action, and it mandates constant learning, evaluation, self-criticism, and a constantly rejuvenated comprehension of a movement's core principles. We believed if we anchored ourselves firmly on that bedrock and used nonviolent action to demonstrate the truth with an unwavering faith, then we could shine a light that would expose the lie of segregation.

We were prepared for what this might mean. We knew that Americans had become so comfortable with misconceptions of separation, inferiority, superiority, and the significance of superficial difference, that many would be very disturbed when exposed to the light of the truth. We knew the brutality of our everyday life was manufactured to corral everyone to submit to an unholy order. We knew this lie would not die easily. But we were also convinced it could never last, so we made a decision to step outside the matrix of everyday life, ground ourselves in the eternal truth, and follow its lead no matter where it took us.

The Civil Rights Movement was more than a struggle over legal rights, it was a spiritual movement led by ministers who wanted to confront the erroneous belief that some of us are more valuable or important than others, and demonstrate the truth of human equality These believers did not debate or fight about this. They did not threaten or mock. They did not malign or degrade their opponents. They simply took action based on the transcendence of unity in an attempt to bear witness to the truth.

Most people today don't understand. It was not only frowned upon but illegal for black people to sit down and eat at a segregated lunch counter. It was against the law for black people and white people to sit next to each other on a public bus. It was illegal for a black person to drink from a water fountain marked WHITE or to sit down in a segregated waiting room at the train or bus station. We believed that if we could find a way to demonstrate that the basis of these regulations was false, the soul of humanity would rise up in righteous indignation and demand that we bring this hypocrisy to an end. The simple act of black and white passengers sitting next to each other on a bus was revolutionary during the Freedom Rides because it confronted a falsehood that had been confirmed by man-made law. It was not the ride itself that was so powerful, but the truth demonstrated by those Riders that was a radical concept in that age.

The March on Washington was powerful because people from all over the country rejected the false boundaries set up by concepts of division and were determined to bear witness to the truth. That truth was crystallized by King's speech that day. The power of his speech was not in the resonance of his voice, the prestige of the platform, or the cadence of his words—it was in the clear truth it articulates.

"I believe that unarmed truth and unconditional love
will have the final word in reality. This is why right, temporarily
defeated, is stronger than evil triumphant."
—MARTIN LUTHER KING JR.

The idea of hundreds of black citizens taking to the streets and marching en masse through downtown Nashville or in Birmingham, Selma, or Washington D.C., was considered drastic because it challenged the muteness of our time and the society that had shut its mouth and turned its head in denial of the truth. Our souls were telling us something was wrong, but the status quo seemed formidable. The narrative of racial segregation had been confirmed for centuries by the skewed deductions of celebrated scientists, by the elegant verses of venerated poets, and the teachings of erudite educators. It had been eloquently defended by politicians and presidents and ferociously enforced by police. It had been sermonized and sanctified by ministers and upheld by the highest courts. Books were written, laws were constructed, and even the word of God was deemed to rationalize separation based on superficial differences. Certainly this mountain of material justified the need to aggressively segregate to avoid the foreboding consequences of race dilution.

The very idea of masses of black people marching on Washington actually struck fear in the hearts of thousands across America. But by taking these actions and confirming our adherence to peace regardless of any negative threats or admonitions raging around us, our insistence on action that was in keeping with the truth became a powerful mirror by which society could see itself. When we took action that belied everything many people thought was true, people began to see their fear for what it was: a mere shadow of reality, a specter that had no substance. And through the protests in the Deep South, where government-sponsored brutality enforced unjust laws, people watching on television could perceive the unseemly consequences of believing a set of distorted facts. They could see the logical conclusion of their irrational fears, and by witnessing the ugly result in others, they were more willing to admit they were wrong. They were more willing to change. By standing in our truth, we affirmed our value and asserted our inalienable right to exist. By marching en masse we were saying: We are not invisible. We are unmistakably real. We are not second-class citizens, but equal and open to all human experience. We do not accept or deserve disdain or abuse. We are human beings, not shuffling or bent, but erect, proud, and standing tall. We are citizens of this nation who have a right to be heard and have a right to fully participate. We were saying we would not be intimidated anymore. We are different, but we are equal.

From my earliest memories, I was fundamentally disturbed by the unbridled meanness of the world around me. Though I was not yet familiar with the words of the Declaration of Independence, I could feel in my bones that segregation was wrong, and I felt I had an obligation to change it.

I was born on a farm in rural Alabama into a family of sharecroppers, who had been working the cotton, corn, and peanut fields of Alabama for generations. Sharecropping took many forms in different states, but mainly it was a system designed to make us fail. Our work was undervalued, our debt inflated, making it almost impossible to get ahead. We were never paid a living wage, so we had to carry punishing debt to buy the necessary tools and supplies we needed in order to farm. To me, it was a vicious cycle I plainly perceived, even as a young boy, was intended to keep us in poverty.

But living on that farm, enveloped by the contrasting purity and innocence of nature, often sequestered from a world that seemed tragically unjust and unfair, I searched inside myself and developed an ability to hear my inner voice speak. As a young boy, I joined the church, because I felt a calling to the ministry at an early age. I knew I wanted to preach, and my first sermon was to the chickens in the barnyard. I loved those gangly, clucking, cooing creatures. To me they seemed so defenseless and so naive. No one ever expected much of them. They were the least respected members of the barnyard. No one tried to distinguish them from one another. They didn't even have names. They were voiceless, anonymous, invisible, and ultimately slaughtered. Perhaps I identified with their jeopardy, but somehow it became my mission as a young boy to offer them dignity and love. I would preach to them to fortify their capacity to be good with a conviction that only a child could have, and I sensed that they heard me. When I would enter the chicken coop, I retreated to a world where unspoken affection was the only currency. The chickens would squawk at first, but then settle down and get very still. We bonded. I loved them, and they loved me back. I would talk to them, try to guide and instruct them, and fuss over them the way my parents, aunts, and uncles fussed over me. I was only about six years old, but I could feel them understanding all of this somehow, and I could tell they were responding to my love in the knowing, reassuring way that animals have. My parents were deeply religious, and I was a boy-preacher in a community of simple people with game-changing faith.

The first time I realized that the world saw me as inferior, a reject, a substandard creation is etched indelibly in my brain. I took a trip to the little town of Troy with my father. Troy was the place he would sell his share of the crops, settle his bills, and purchase new supplies. At six years old, this should have been a moment of pride for me. It was my first trip into town, a big deal for a country boy. It made me feel a bit older and a little more important to go on this journey with my dad. But the moment I left the nurturing circle of my community, my glee was slammed by the steel fist of hate. When we got to town, I could not help but notice the demeaning way my father was treated. He was the man I looked up to, loved, and respected, but he was assaulted by words and abuse, called "boy," addressed by his first name, directed to submit to the worst violence and dared to mount any defense.

And then there were the signs that dotted the entrances to so many businesses up and down Main Street. They screamed out a degradation that pursued me like a clanging indictment of my existence: WHITE WOMEN, COLORED WOMEN, WHITE MEN, COLORED MEN, WHITE WAITING, COLORED WAITING. My skin color was a part of me I could never change, a characteristic I did not choose and was not responsible for, so this derision seemed hopeless to contain. It was as though the whole world was shouting out that I was defective, somehow poorly made.

Those signs were humiliating—painful symbols that the world around me denied my worth.

Years later, as a teenager in high school, I remember reading about the U.S. Supreme Court decision on *Brown v. The Board of Education of Topeka* in the newspaper. The news stories seemed to suggest that the public schools would at last be integrated. I wanted to jump for joy. Every day I would rumble and bump on an old broken-down school bus over the dirt roads in my neck of the woods to the smoothness of the paved roads in the city. There I would see white children glide by on nice, clean buses that dropped them off at big, impressive buildings made of brick or stone; some even had columns. There were dozens of classrooms in those schools, an upstairs and downstairs, new books, and all kinds of facilities to help students learn.

I was dying for the same opportunity to get a good education, so I was incredibly excited this law had finally passed. Even though I lived in a segregated environment it had not dampened the natural attraction and curiosity children have for one another. My enthusiasm was not only about scholastic opportunity, but the excitement of making new friends. I saw so many students around my age, I wanted to talk to them, find out what they were like. In my heart I felt there was so much that we could share. Every day after I read about the

Brown decision I kept expecting that one day when I climbed onto my school bus I might see some white students on board or maybe a new friend might just sit down beside me. He or she might attend my school or I might be transferred to theirs. The prospects were really exciting. I kept waiting and waiting but nothing ever happened. After a while, it became very clear that it was just business as usual in my little corner of Alabama. Life went on as though the *Brown* decision never happened. My expectation faded into the blur of everyday life.

Sometimes I think leaders today don't realize how people hang on their words. People don't want a handout most of the time. They just want a little help. They want the people who represent them to use a little power and a little influence to help them solve some of the problems of their community. And in the fifty years I have spent in public life, I've met many people who are deeply concerned and who are trying to make a difference. I've also met many who I would say love the world, but don't actually like people. Some of them become leaders among leaders, charged to speak for the very people they don't understand, and their hearts are hardened to the struggles facing the people they represent.

In so many ways I see that disconnection from the day-to-day life of ordinary people hampering politics today. There are leaders who truly believe that, despite the worst recession in eighty years, the unemployed could find work if they just weren't so lazy, that the poor made critical errors that condemn them to their misfortune, that inner city youth have a lesser capacity to learn, and that the elderly should be tasked to plan better for their decline. There are leaders who seem to worship the rich as though they are more worthy of privilege, more deserving of forgiveness, more justified in their mistakes than ordinary Americans. These leaders are completely disconnected from the truth of the lives of most Americans, and they hold to these misconceptions regardless of the facts. I do not know how they can ignore rising poverty, extended unemployment, food lines beginning to emerge in some states, whole families living in cars and panel trucks, and seniors choosing between medication and food. I am not sure what kind of blindness sets in, but there is still a grand denial based on the belief in the separateness of human experience that is unwilling to conform to the truth.

The truth is that we are all interrelated. There would be no rich without poor, no healing without the sick, no young without the old, no "first world" country without the "third world" country. We are all "inextricably linked," King said, and that is why it is futile for any group to draw lines in the sand. The vast sea of truth will merely wash those weak lines away. The preference for segregation is still rampant in our world, in so many ways. The Civil Rights Movement helped us rid ourselves of legalized discrimination, a particularly pernicious form of segregation, but our desire to exclude ourselves from one another, critique each other's worthiness, and take exception to whom we should speak, cast our eyes upon, or admit into our circle is based on myriad rules that govern our civility or our disdain.

What will it take for each of us to learn from the lessons of segregation and separation and apply them liberally to our own lives? If we are truly to learn the lessons of the Civil Rights Movement, the Holocaust, or the conflict in Northern Ireland, we must concede that discomfort breeds dislike, dislike breeds disdain, disdain breeds contempt, and contempt breeds hate. We cannot afford to relegate the victories in the struggle between love and hate to one group or another, whether they happen on American shores or not. The truth is, as long as we see life in terms of its duality, instead of its commonality, our lives will always demand we overcome.

We say that we want our leaders to tell us the truth, but are we prepared to make the sacrifices required once we hear that truth? Many candidates are afraid to speak the truth because they believe the people will reject the tough adjustments that might be called for—a cutback on services, a hike in taxes, a decision to put a halfway house in your neighborhood, to thin the population of urban deer, to close schools or military bases, or to lay people off. In order to get elected, many strategists actually recommend hiding the truth by using vague language or feel-good facts. The best approach, they would say, is to resurrect the old, familiar ghosts of our past. They are comfortable, nonthreatening, and fulfill the people's need to verify the legends that support our national image of ourselves.

Thus, it is not only the politicians, but the people, also, who participate in this grand denial because they don't stay engaged and informed. They allow others to interpret the facts for them. They do no independent research. They are exhausted by critical thinking, yet they feel betrayed when they are confronted by corruption in politics that shatters their illusions. Politicians have a fiduciary responsibility to preserve the public's trust. That goes without saying, and they are responsible when they lie or break the law. But the citizens of a democracy also have a responsibility to remain engaged and informed so they cannot be easily duped. How many man-on-the-street interviews have we seen with reasonable Americans who have no idea who the president is, don't know what the president's cabinet does, or the names of their own representatives? It is much harder to govern in a complex democracy when the people are uninformed.

And when brave, principled politicians do tell the truth, too many times they are attacked and vilified. The people don't always want to accept the mandate the truth represents. When the people judge their representatives mainly on superficial criteria and not on the issues, it leaves more room for pretenders who talk a good game, who appear likeable and "down" with the people, to get the job. When we base our decisions mainly on superficial data, we cannot afford to be surprised when our trust is periodically betrayed. There was a time when a man or woman who considered integrity more important than getting reelected was seen as virtuous and principled. Today, no one even mentions the idea of virtue or principle, let alone aspires to develop these values. Now it's all about the game, playing it hard and playing it smart not telling the truth. A lie is not contemptible in these times, if it can be used to get ahead. Perhaps that is why we have had to suffer through so many jarring revelations in our society: journalists who fabricate stories, employees who lie about their credentials, a strategically miscalculated rush to war, clergy and coaches who rob children of their youth, and politicians who feign morality but are bought and sold. Gandhi would say that all exploitation or victimization is based on the cooperation, either knowing or unwitting, of the oppressed.

The old foe of separation still runs rampant in a

game-playing society. A belief in the game suggests there is no relationship between the hoodwinked and the deceiver. The robber barons of today's mortgage fraud might have believed they got away with millions, but the tanking of our economy devalues all they stole. Nothing can break that inextricable bond between us all. Consequences can be delayed, maybe even softened, but not avoided. If one goes up, we can all rise. But if many fall, the height of the summit will be diminished.

People depend on their leadership to help maintain stability and peace. The most vulnerable, the most susceptible people in our society especially deserve the truth. It took a long time for me to truly understand why nothing changed in my world after the *Brown* decision. But once I discovered the truth, I was prepared to give my life to revolution.

Segregation aggravated so many who experienced it, but those who stayed in Alabama found a way to manage their vexation. I never could. It rubbed me the wrong way all the time. I was not so much angry as deeply disappointed at the meanness that weighed down all my interactions with the outside world. Today I see that sadness in the eyes of the hungry children of Somalia, the trafficked girls of India or Russia, all the children growing up in conflict zones, and so many others suffering the worst this world has to offer. These children have radiance, but their eyes reveal injustices they witness but cannot terminate in their imagination. In the few pictures I have of my childhood, even as a little boy, I am not smiling and joyful, though I experienced many happy times. Even at a young age, I can see the pensive question in my eyes as I strained to understand why it had to be this way.

I never let sadness get the best of me, though. People often say, "John, you are too optimistic." They think I am too hopeful, unrealistic, even naive. But I see myself as a believer who has witnessed the evolution of what others believed would never change.

Some would say the goal of our activism was legislative victory, but that is more a conclusion drawn from the outcome of the movement, rather than from the ideas that deeply motivated us. We had been denied our civil liberties for so long that we did not expect the government to be fair or to grant what we were demanding. Our primary goal was to emerge from the shaded confines of a lie and walk freely in the light of the truth.

Even though we had been rejected by society, we believed that all people had the capacity to be good. We believed not only we, but the perpetrators of violence, were victims as well, who began their lives in innocence but were taught to hate, abuse, and draw distinctions between themselves and others. We held no malice toward them and believed in the power of the truth to penetrate that negative conditioning and remind people of their innocence once again. We focused on the end we hoped to see and kept our eyes on that prize. We could not waste time harboring bitterness or resentment. We knew that our focus had to be on what we hoped to create, not the indignities we were pressing to leave behind. Hating our aggressors was like looking back when we wanted to move forward. We had to use our energy to manifest our dreams, and entertaining animosity would have given more power to the status quo.

If we truly believed in oneness, then we could not allow ourselves to engage in the same violence as our wayward brothers and sisters. Though some might justify any retaliation in light of the brutality we faced, we asked where retribution ends and wanton violence begins. We could not use the tactics we hoped to eradicate, or we would be no better than those committing crimes against us. Instead we decided to use the truth as a sword to penetrate the rationale of injustice and awaken the consciousness of a society that had looked the other way. That is the main reason we were particular about the way we dressed, because we wanted to be identified as upstanding citizens. The men wore suits and ties while the women looked dignified in conservative dresses. We had to be seen the way most Americans viewed themselves, helping to bridge the gap between any stereotype that perceived us as different and the truth that we were not.

Our method of demonstration in many instances was the sit-in because it was a simple, nonviolent act that illustrated the harmlessness of human connection, the innocence of sharing a meal at a lunch counter or a seat on a bus. The sit-in exposed the absurdity of barring the natural ability of people to flow to one another, and it revealed the monstrous, outlandish fear that had accumulated over centuries of compliance with injustice. Society had drawn a line in the sand, and we crossed it without apology.

Our approach was not passive, as some people believed; it was uncompromising. Southerners saw it as forward and aggressive. Based on Mohandas Gandhi's fundamental tactic, *satyagraha,* which means holding to the truth, or more literally, insistence on the truth, the sit-in confronted society and forced it to look in the mirror at its own reflection. Through our own independent study and our guided workshops with Rev. Jim Lawson, a man many called the mystic of the movement, we came to recognize that the pain of our social experience was in part due to our own acceptance of it. We all bore the psychic wounds of racism embedded in our being. This was no fault of our own. Blame was not the issue. Centuries of conditioning assured our compliance, and it was critical that we engage in a process that allowed us to perceive our complicity with this malicious order. Then we would be freed from knee-jerk responses to the hatred we had so intimately known, freed to map out our alliance with the truth.

As citizens, we knew we had ceded some of our individual rights to society in order to live together as a community. But we did not believe this social contract included support for an immoral system. Since the people invested government with its authority, we understood that we had to obey the law. But when law became suppressive and tyrannical, when human law violated divine principles, we felt it was not only our right, but our duty to disobey. As Henry Thoreau strongly believed, to comply with an unjust system is to accept abuse. It is not the role of the citizen to follow the government down a path that violates his or her own conscience.

This, in our estimation, was not a valid expression of our consent to be governed, so we were obliged to find a way to align our souls with the truth. Violence was not an option because it exemplified the very wrong we were seeking to correct, and it was not a rational, strategic choice because it met our opponents on their territory where they would surely dominate. Nonviolent noncooperation through the sit-in, the stand-in, through the protest march, was the most eloquent way we could signal our resistance to what was wrong and assert what was right. We believed that if we held strong, regardless of beatings, arrests, or jailings, the divine spark that is in all of us would bear witness to the truth. And the soul of each witness would wrestle with its own conscience and demand to be reconciled with the truth.

THEY THREW EVERYTHING at us in the sixties in an attempt to deny the validity of our reality. They called us Communists and hippies, outside agitators and troublemakers. They infiltrated us and investigated us. They floated false rumors and negative propaganda. They ran us down with horses and bludgeoned us with billy clubs and baseball bats. They jailed us, they beat us, they bombed us, and sprayed us with tear gas and fire hoses. They even assassinated a president, a candidate, and a King. President John F. Kennedy, Robert Kennedy, and Martin Luther King Jr. were three symbols of hope. They were three men, three leaders who were sensitive to the truth.

Those two brothers began their term as president and attorney general without a real understanding of the problems of race in the South. But through the protests and the demonstrations they came to understand how deeply we suffered.

They began to hear the mandate to address the very hypocrisy Dr. King spoke about. These men grew. They changed because of what they experienced, and that is all you can ask of another person. Don't close your eyes because you are afraid of what you will see. Be honest in your assessment. Transformation and revelation require an adjustment from what we know to what we know can be.

Had President Kennedy lived, I don't know what would have happened. I met him only a few times before he was killed, but I do know that in the time I interacted with him, he changed. He was not locked into one game plan or partisan agenda. He was interested in the human agenda, and he wanted to serve. There is no doubt he was a shrewd politician. He was what he called a pragmatic idealist, but he was also a good man who defined success as the ability to use his political skill to conform the convoluted ways of politics to the mandate of what was right.

I got to know Bobby Kennedy very well. I worked on his presidential campaign and in fact I was with him in California. I had seen him minutes before his speech and was in the Ambassador Hotel watching when we heard the news that he had been shot. Had he lived, I believe he would have been elected president. I think this nation would have followed a different course, leading us to a more humane, sustainable democracy. People have said he was a tough, sharp-tongued attorney general, but I saw him grow to be so much more. Bobby had passion. When he became aware of the plight of the common man, he applied his passion to our defense. The loss of his brother and his growing awareness through the movement of the tragic disenfranchisement of the poor gave him a compassion I have rarely seen in any politician to this day.

On the campaign trail Bobby purposely veered off the beaten track to visit Americans in their hometowns, to see for himself the conditions of the people he hoped to lead. He went to the Mississippi Delta, to the hills of Kentucky. He visited farm workers in the fields of California to see their faces and look them in the eyes. He showed them he was a man of the people who was not afraid to stand with them where they lived and he asked to be their champion in the fight to lift them up. I loved Bobby Kennedy. I loved him for his ability to be vulnerable, to be touched and moved, for his ability to throw open his heart and discover a connection to all humankind. In his brother's eulogy, Edward Kennedy said this about Bobby: "My brother need not be idealized, or enlarged in death beyond what he was in life; to be remembered simply as a good and decent man, who saw wrong and tried to right it, saw suffering and tried to heal it, saw war and tried to stop it." I think this is a legacy to which we should all aspire.

Of all the leaders in the movement, Martin Luther King Jr. was closest in age to me, so he was like my big brother. He was also my hero. If it had not been for Martin Luther King Jr., I don't know where I would be today. I would probably not be a member of Congress. I might still be in Alabama picking cotton, preaching to the chickens, and railing against the oppression that was consuming me. Martin Luther King Jr. taught an entire generation how to speak truth to power, how to stand up, speak out, and speak up for what was principled and right. He taught us how to defend our human dignity, how to struggle for a higher cause, yet his message was love and his method was creative nonviolent resistance to evil. He exemplified with his life a moral path to follow that has eternal power, and his words and his legacy have inspired legions of people struggling for freedom all around the world.

That is why it is so fitting and so appropriate that he be honored today on the National Mall because he freed not just a people, but an entire nation from the burden of hate. Through his leadership, people young and old, black and white, from different parts of America and from nations around the world were able to expose the falsehood of division, the idea that there is a separation between us that makes one person somehow better than the other. The stain of this lie had permeated American history and was embedded in the fabric of American life, not just in the South but across the country. His leadership and his activism helped to redeem the soul of America, a nation destined for greatness but tarnished by a persistent, nagging untruth. This one man became the symbol of the need to build a true democracy in America, and that is why he stands in the shadow of America's greatest presidents, within the line of sight to the monuments to George Washington, Thomas Jefferson, and Abraham Lincoln. He was never elected to any public office. He was a simple preacher from Atlanta, Georgia, but he transformed an entire nation by standing on the power of the truth.

I KNEW THESE three young men. I loved them, and they were shot down in the battle for justice. When they died I mourned. I knew my life would never be the same. So many people I knew simply dropped out and disappeared. Some I never saw again. To this day, I still feel it is my moral obligation, as one person who knew them all, who still has a vote on the floor of the House, to ask myself when I have to make a tough decision, "What would Martin do? What would Bobby Kennedy do in this situation?" Each person must find his or her own inner compass, the thing one turns to when trying to distinguish truth from lies, and right from wrong.

Despite everything that has happened, regardless of the pain of their loss, despite all the other nonviolent peaceful warriors who suffered and sometimes fell, I have never once considered giving up or giving out. I could not let myself get lost in a sea of despair, because I had faith that the truth is bigger than all humanity. The tragedy of their loss was a crisis of faith, but in that struggle I discovered that you can kill a Medgar Evers or a Jimmie Lee Jackson. You can kill three civil rights workers named Chaney, Goodman, and Schwerner. You can bomb four innocent little girls in church on a Sunday morning. You can even kill three of the finest leaders of the twentieth century, but you cannot kill the truth they represented. The truth marches on; it is not connected to the life of any one individual. When a person dies, the dream does not die. You can kill a man, but the truth that he stood for will never die.

Each one of these people sacrificed their lives for the truth, and each death, each loss prevailed upon every one of us in this nation to put away the lies of segregation and separation and come closer to the truth. And it lives today in the hearts and minds of young people who have no comprehension of the lie that characterized American society just a few decades ago. They cannot even understand it. Society has moved in the direction of greater unity to the degree that young people today cannot even comprehend the spiritual struggle of the sixties. It bewilders and befuddles them that it was once illegal for two people to sit down next to each other on a public bus, sleep in the same hotel, or share a meal together. Sometimes when I tell these stories to little children, they begin to cry because they can feel the pain of that injustice. In the end, the truth obliterated an illusion that people paid with their own souls to uphold. That is why I say Martin Luther King Jr. and the Civil Rights Movement liberated not just a people, but an entire nation from the degradation of hostility and hate. Some resent the national holiday in Martin's name, and question whether he deserves a memorial on the National Mall. I see it as a testament to the truth he represented. It will stand as a symbol of a man and a movement that injected new meaning, as he would say, into the very veins of civilization.

We have come a long way, but there is still a great deal of work to do. There is still too much separation and division, too much hatred and discrimination in our nation and our world today. But the presence of evil does not negate the power of the good. When people ask me whether the Civil Rights Movement was successful in light of all the attempts to turn back the clock, I can answer affirmatively, without a doubt. As much of our work was grounded in truth, it will stand the test of time. It was never our job to save all of humankind, but to do what we could to rescue ourselves and our generation from the confining illusions of hate. And by doing so, we served all of humankind. We were one radiant light that did shine, and others, electrified by the cause of freedom, must follow their own light of truth. Each generation must do its part for freedom to ring.

"There are only two mistakes one can make along the road to truth; not going all the way, and not starting."
—BUDDHA

Each person must act according to the dictates of his or her conscience. You must search for the truth, seek it out. Do not allow yourself to be blown by the prevailing winds of our time, but try your best to reach down to the core, to the central foundation of the truth.

Through a time of struggle or difficulty, you must hold on to the principles that define you, and when all else fails, just hold on. People have asked me, "What happened to the dream?" I say to them and I say to you, "The dream is us."

My fellow civil rights protestors and I (right) vote on our next moves in Montgomery, Alabama in 1961. *Photo credit: Bruce Davidson/Magnum Photos*

Concerned for the safety of protestors after several of us—myself included (pictured with bandage)—were attacked by angry mobs, Dr. Martin Luther King Jr. speaks out about the violence to the media in Montgomery, Alabama in 1961. *Photo credit: Bruce Davidson/Magnum Photos*

I (second from left) demonstrate with others in 1962 by kneeling in prayer at the Cairo, Illinois pool, which did not allow blacks. *Photo credit: Danny Lyon/ Magnum Photos*

As the new chairman of the Student Nonviolent Coordinating Committee (SNCC), I was the sixth speaker at in the transformative March on Washington on August 28, 1963. Dr. King was the ninth. *Photo credit: Danny Lyon/Magnum Photos*

President Kennedy welcomes the speakers and leaders of the March on Washington to the White House. He greeted each of us at the door of the Oval Office, saying, "You did a good job." To Dr. King, he said, "you did a good job, and you had a dream." *Photo credit: Courtesy of the Library of Congress (LC-DIG-ds-04413)*

Less than one month after the success of the March on Washington we had to face the tragic bombing of the Sixteenth Street Baptist Church in Montgomery. Here I am (third from right) with Julian Bond, Jimmy Hicks, and Jeremiah X, looking at the damage to the church from across the street. Four little girls were killed that day. *Photo credit: Danny Lyon/Magnum Photos*

At any SNCC meeting a member might spur us to break into song to encourage our spirits or express our sense of celebration. Here we are singing in a meeting led by SNCC Executive Secretary James Forman during the tumultuous winter of 1963–1964. *Photo credit: Danny Lyon/Magnum Photos*

Top Southern Christian Leadership Conference (SCLC) members Hosea Williams (far left) and Andrew Young, meet with reporters alongside me (second from left) on March 7, 1965, before we begin the first Selma to Montgomery March. *Photo credit: Spider Martin*

I was struck on the head with nightsticks by Alabama state troopers during the first Selma March. At the time, I thought it might be my last protest, but I lived to continue the struggle. *Photo credit: Spider Martin*

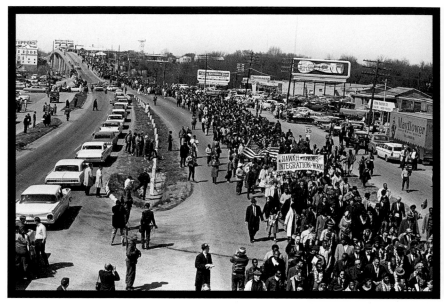

Many of us at the final march wore beautiful leis brought from the Hawaii delegation. I am pictured at the very bottom, with Dr. King and Rev. Abernathy in that same row, third and fourth from the right. This view of thousands of marchers continues to inspire me. *Photo credit: Spider Martin*

(From left) I, Martin Luther King Jr., and the civil rights leaders Ralph Abernathy, James Bevel, and Andrew Young lead protestors down Highway 80 at the start of the third and final Selma to Montgomery march. *Photo credit: Spider Martin*

On the final Selma to Montgomery march, Martin Luther King Jr., other protestors, and I walk past an antebellum mansion behind which slave quarters remained standing nearly a century after the end of the Civil War. *Photo credit: Spider Martin*

My colleagues in Congress and I stand on the steps of the U.S. Capitol in 2013 and remember September 11th in an annual ceremony. *Photo credit: Courtesy of Rep. John Lewis*

I lead a commemoration at the Capitol of the 50th anniversary of the March on Washington, honoring the crucial role Congress played during the March. *Photo credit: Courtesy of Rep. John Lewis*

I speak at a news conference at the U.S. Capitol in memory of the victims of the Orlando nightclub shootings. I love that slogan: Disarm Hate. That's what nonviolence is all about.
Photo credit: Courtesy of the Human Rights Campaign

One of the proudest moments of my life: President Barack Obama awards me the Presidential Medal of Freedom in 2010. *Photo credit: Michael Collopy*

ACT

"Our lives begin to end the day we become
silent about things that matter."
—MARTIN LUTHER KING JR.

Most of what is taught about Dr. King is that he had a dream, but I can tell you Martin Luther King Jr. was much more than a dreamer. He believed that faith had no meaning unless it had the power to resolve the problems of our daily lives. King was a great preacher, yes, but he also climbed down from the pulpit to practice what he preached. He lived according to the dictates of his conscience, and he was guided by a drive to accomplish a far-reaching goal—to redeem the soul of America. This is a nation still scarred by the violence of slavery, including the forms of legalized segregation and racial discrimination we faced almost one hundred years after the end of the Civil War. Dr. King never stopped pressing toward that goal of redemption. He never sold out for lesser rewards.

Today many people believe that accumulating wealth certifies their success. Yet, there are very few people admired in history for the accumulation of wealth alone. American moguls like Andrew Carnegie or Andrew Mellon, even those living today—Bill Gates or David Rubenstein—reach for philanthropy as a way to give meaning to their wealth. They do not value wealth as a final cap on their accomplishments. Rather, their contributions to bettering society earn them respect and lasting recognition because those contributions reflect the philanthropist's courage, generosity, integrity, and sacrifice—all expressions of love for humankind or a higher cause. Most of the participants in the Civil Rights Movement never achieved great wealth. Even its most notable leader, Dr. King, never attained immense fortune, yet he is the only person in American history commemorated on the National Mall along with presidents and the founders of this nation.

When he was awarded the Nobel Peace Prize in 1964, Dr. King was granted about $54,123—a hefty sum back then, equal to almost half a million dollars today. He could have kept that money and given his family a much more comfortable life. God knows they deserved it. In King's autobiography, compiled from notes and research gathered by Dr. Claybourne Carson, he talks about one late night in Montgomery when he was paralyzed by fear and pure desperation. He was burdened by work that often took him away from home into the grip of a perilous hatred. While he was away, his wife and children—then one toddler and a newborn baby—were bombarded constantly by menacing phone calls. His family lived in turmoil, fearing he might be arrested, attacked, or injured. Every time he left home his wife could never be certain he would return. That was not the life he had wanted for his beautiful wife and little children. He was racked by guilt that he might be failing them, dragging them into a terrifying reality. The money from the Nobel Prize could have helped buy their way out of constant jeopardy. Those prize winnings were more than enough for him to buy a fine home away from the tensions his young family had to endure.

They could have moved up North, where prejudice still existed, but where his family would have been spared from a world of fear. Instead, he dug in. He donated every penny to the Civil Rights Movement. He believed that if the work succeeded, millions of Americans, including his children and his children's children, would be liberated from the terrorism of hate. He was motivated by the desire to win a victory for humanity, not by desire for his own personal comfort. After he died, his wife Coretta remained in Atlanta in the same home for years. They were both committed to living as members of their community and no fame or fortune could pull them from it. They were participants in the struggle. *None are free until all are free.* That was their faith and motto.

Intersectionality, the call of many young activists today, was also a fundamental, yet often overlooked, part of Dr. King's action plan. His focus was not restricted to legislative advances, though, after his death, the power of government was used to implement an interpretation of his vision. He would have marveled at the political, economic, and social progress those changes ushered in, but what he hoped for was comprehensive, not confined to civil or legal rights. He sought economic justice, true equality, environmental justice, labor rights, political power, social acceptance, and respect for the dignity of all humankind.

He wanted poor and working people of all ethnicities and faiths, from every region of the country, to join together across the boundaries constructed to divide us. He realized that we were all struggling against different aspects of the same oppression. Race was a false limit, meant to impede coalition between groups that together could stand up to and defeat the violators of human dignity. The forces that oppressed Latino farmworkers with starvation wages and cruel working conditions were the same forces that denied white coal miners, autoworkers, and meatpackers safe working conditions and living wages. As a Baptist minister, King had a vision of intersectionality that led him to appeal to the conscience of Catholic priests, white Protestant pastors, and Jewish rabbis, among other religious leaders. His last action was the development of a Poor People's Campaign, which united individuals across racial, political, social, and religious barriers to stand up as a unified force against oppression and injustice.

Even though Dr. King was killed before he could put into practice all he envisioned, his "dream" has transformed our society. Though we may experience setbacks, we still live in a less separated, more unified America than ever before, an America that is very different from the one I experienced when I was young. Legalized segregation is gone to such a degree that the young children I talk to today cannot even imagine the America I grew up in. They cannot understand it when I tell them that a person could be put in jail for sleeping under the same hotel roof as a black person. I have seen little children cry when I describe the humiliations of sitting at the back of the bus and only a few of the hostilities we endured. They simply cannot comprehend how a system that was so irrational and inhumane could exist in the United States.

This discomfort people express when they hear the truth about our history means that the Civil Rights Movement not only changed laws but human hearts as well. The same young children I meet today might have been some of the children taken by their parents to witness Ku Klux Klan lynchings and cross burnings. Most would have been conformed to the attitudes and conventions of segregation by teachers, police officers, parents, and even ministers who believed in a necessary division among the races. I speak to hundreds of children every year, and the fact that many are bewildered by my descriptions of legalized segregation represents tremendous progress.

The human heart is the most important frontier to conquer in the struggle for human dignity. Once the heart is softened, shifts in social norms are seen as logical and rational. The movement to legalize gay marriage is an excellent example of action that successfully used a directed, strategic approach to reach the human heart. Of course, the legal advocacy that led to the landmark US Supreme Court decision on gay marriage, *Obergefell v. Hodges*, as well as decades of legislative lobbying, were also cornerstones of this shift. But strategists recognized that even if judges and legislators saw the legal sensibility of change, it would be difficult for them to defend their decisions without a widespread shift in American attitudes. This is a major task, but advocates of gay marriage did not shrink from the challenge. They took it on. They found ways to humanize the issue, to use the true stories of dedicated, committed gay couples who could not participate in a partner's medical care, death wishes, health insurance plans, and so forth as a way to demonstrate the reasons why civil marriage was a humane choice.

Once people began to realize that gay marriage affected their sons and daughters, mothers and fathers, they embraced the need to make a more compassionate choice in our society. That is why it gained such widespread support—not total acceptance, mind you—but enough support to make dramatic changes. Many began to see the issue of gay marriage as a family matter—something that affected people they loved and touched their own personal lives—not as a court decision or a legislative mandate. That is the one great advantage the gay rights movement has. Many of us have gay friends, family members, celebrity favorites, coworkers, or associates. Grandchildren began talking to their grandparents and great-grandparents about the issue. Children began explaining what was wrong with current policy to their parents, aunts, and uncles, calling for greater humanity in America law. Those kitchen table discussions were at the center of an undeniable shift in American attitudes, so much so that the Supreme Court—one of the most conservative in decades—ruled in favor of gay marriage.

This need to humanize an issue is critical to every movement. In activism, try to aim your most powerful action at the emotional resistance held in the heart, the beliefs that lead people to view a human problem as though it were alien. Ask yourself what action or series of actions you could design that would unravel this hardened thinking for those who hold those notions. Put yourself in their shoes or survey their attitudes to try to understand why people are so defensive and fearful of having their guns taken away, for example, or why they choose to vote against their own interests. Once you comprehend how they think and feel, it is easier to come up with an approach that helps them see the human face of an issue.

The greatest resistance to comprehensive immigration reform, for example, is the distance of most Americans from the immigrant experience. American parents don't have to live fearing that immigration agents might deport their children when they go to school or detain their parents while they are waiting at a traffic light. Most Americans will never know this kind of terror. Humanizing that issue, sensitizing people to the horror associated with this deportation policy, is the key to overcoming resistance to immigration reform. To me there is no such thing as an illegal human being, but my background makes me acutely aware of the devastating consequences rounding up and deporting millions of immigrants would have on our society, especially since this nation has done it before.

The Mexican Revolution in the early 1900s motivated immigration to America, but many Mexicans came at the request of big corporations to work on the extension of American railroads into the Southwest and to work in American manufacturing—in steel mills, in meatpacking plants, and in agriculture. Big business had directly asked the Mexican government to send willing, lower-cost workers to this country. The labor movement was having a substantial impact on the American factory system around that time. A major push to organize labor had begun in the 1800s, so by the beginning of the twentieth century, labor had become a powerful force in American industry and politics.

A strong progressive movement was also underway. Robert "Fighting Bob" LaFollette was elected to the U.S. Senate on the Progressive Party ticket, the women's suffrage movement had successfully won passage of the Nineteenth Amendment in 1920, and labor unions were beginning to gain significant power in American business and politics. Nearly 150 garment workers, trapped in an unsafe building at New York's Triangle Shirtwaist factory, died when the factory caught fire in 1911, and that disaster led to more workplace-safety regulations. Massive strikes across a variety of industries were imposing worker demands on big business, requiring companies to allocate a portion of their profits to modifications to ensure worker safety, raise wages, shorten working hours, and create conditions that lifted workers out of poverty. Many of the concessions demanded by the labor movement are considered standard practice in our country today, but it required activism and organization to make that happen. Paid sick leave, retirement pensions, the forty-hour workweek, lunch hours, restrictions on child labor, safety and hygienic practices in factories and businesses—all the everyday norms of contemporary American worklife—stem from the hard-won struggles of labor unions. Finally, the heightened scrutiny surrounding the Teapot Dome scandal in 1922, involving unscrupulous activities by oil companies in collusion with President Warren G. Harding's administration, led corporate leaders to seek an unregulated, cheaper workforce. So they requested that America open its borders to Mexican workers.

But when the stock market crashed in 1929, nativist feelings began to surge to the forefront. Racist ideas took hold and Mexicans were forcibly rounded up and deported back to their country to "free up" opportunities for those who had been born here. A half million to two million Mexicans were sent back south of the border. Most of those who were rounded up were actually naturalized American citizens, and some had even been born in this country. They were all deported to Mexico, without regard to their citizenship status. People pushing for comprehensive immigration reform must educate and sensitize Americans to the inhumane nature of these deportation procedures. Most Americans tend to believe that only "offenders" would be vulnerable to government-sponsored violence, but action must be taken to demonstrate that that is not true. They must find ways to make others walk in the shoes of immigrant families—including women and little children, detained in American prisons—to comprehend the misery endured by people whose only crime is to seek a better life. Many spend weeks in solitary confinement once they get here; some even die under suspicious circumstances in federal custody. Once activists demonstrate, by some effective, creative means, the inhumane treatment of immigrants they can get movement on immigration reform.

African Americans can easily identify with these struggles because they face similar problems. It was not until the Black Lives Matter protests began to call attention to the brutal treatment of black teenage boys that there was any concern about the state- or city-sponsored carnage in our communities. This was true even though Amnesty International and Human Rights Watch had reported for years that the United States had the highest prison population in the world, even above countries led by communist dictators or nations wracked by war. BLM protests began making people aware that African American men and boys were being brutalized in police custody and sent to prison for half their lives for low-level offenses. Mass demonstrations highlighted an injustice most Americans were not aware of and led them to look more closely at our system of incarceration. Members of Congress, legal and corrections experts, and researchers were aware of the problem, but it was not until the Black Lives Matter protests heightened awareness that people began to even consider change. Sensitization is one of the key benefits of protest. It makes people aware that there is a problem that requires the attention of our democracy. However, protest is not an end in itself. If it's the only strategy a movement brings to bear on a social problem, it loses its impact. It must be employed as a means to some specific end and as a building block of an entire campaign.

BLM protests helped educate people about the different challenges every African American faces. They helped bring to light "the talk," a discussion most black parents have with their male children, across socioeconomic boundaries, about how to deal with the police. Many Americans realized that the mere existence of this mandatory discussion across class lines meant black families, even affluent black families, had to face a reality they did not understand. This kernel of information connected to the deep human need to keep their children safe. Because many parents had never had to have "the talk" with their children, they began to grasp how dire the situation was. In this way, protest has been an excellent educational tool.

However, in order to stem the rising tide of police brutality and the militarization of the police, regulations inside police departments must be changed. Police academies must use different training methods. A massive education campaign is needed for those who might sit on juries and for those writing laws that protect police but permit the murder of defenseless teenagers to continue unchecked. More independent investigations of these crimes may need to be conducted by outside groups, like the NAACP or legal defense organizations, so that activism is based on sound proof. To rely on the police to provide evidence that would implicate some in their own ranks might be asking too much in many cities. Also, teams of lawyers must research legal strategies so that prosecutors who are willing to indict police—and parents who are defending the rights of their slain children—are armed with the legal arguments they need to win cases, instead of losing them. Activists must also find ways to demonstrate the innocence of these victims. Somehow, Americans were horrified by the way an Asian physician was dragged off a plane, but they are able to normalize the deaths of hundreds of black teenagers. People automatically suspect blacks of wrongdoings that lead to their deaths. They do not believe or even see our little children as innocent. The seven-year-old sister of Tamir Rice, a twelve-year-old boy who was shot and killed by Cleveland police while he was playing with a toy gun, was also shot when she simply rushed to her brother's side. Our society cannot yet see the inhumanity of this because they see these black children as some kind of threat, even when they're only doing things that other children do. Those fighting for change in these laws will also have to craft strategies that break through a hardness of heart that does not perceive the innocence of black children or as people who deserve our protection, instead of our punishment.

The reason the Civil Rights Movement is looked to as a blueprint for change is that it employed a concerted collection of activist strategies so effectively that in about twelve years it transformed laws, attitudes, and traditions in this country that my parents and their elders thought would never change. Though we still are far from liberated, there is no question that American consciousness is different today than it was decade ago. It changed the relationship between people and government, so that government became a sympathetic referee in the struggles of the poor, the disenfranchised, and working people. The middle class grew as a result of government initiatives that opened opportunities to buy a home, to go to school, even the best schools, to develop a small business, and to gain wealth. These options freed the working class to buy access to the middle class, and helped poor people move from one economic strata to the next. The idea that government should lift up the conditions of the masses of Americans was one of the key contributions of the civil rights era. The movement helped generate a greater commitment to democracy in our republic than ever before.

Dr. King used to say that nothing can stop the marching feet of a committed and determined people armed with an idea whose time has come. No government, no multinational corporation, no agency at all could counter the mandates of a unified world community. And that is why so much energy and resources are invested in division and separation. Throughout American and even world history, there has often been systematic, coordinated resistance to true democracy. That is because the unity of the people is the most powerful force in the world. Imagine what we could accomplish if all 7.5 billion people on this planet, or even the 326 million people in this country alone, decided to unite to take coordinated action on a single issue. Imagine what we could accomplish if we decided that, together, we would combat world hunger, call a halt to violence in our cities, end all war, cut off the drug trade, or stop the spread of disease.

In high school many study *The Social Contract* developed by Jean-Jacques Rousseau, a Swiss philosopher influenced by other thinkers like John Locke and Thomas Hobbes (both from England), as well as Immanuel Kant of Germany and others during Europe's Age of Enlightenment or Age of Reason in the eighteenth century. This was a period when many of the modern ideas of democracy were born in the West.

Of course, many African and Native American traditional cultures are rooted in democratic principles and many democratic ideals of ancient Greece and Rome emerged from the writings in the Great Library in Alexandria, Egypt. So the idea of government being accountable to the people is an ancient concept.

However, in its modern form, Rousseau asserts that in order for government to exist at all, there is an implied agreement between the people and its government. The people agree to give up a part of their free will—the right to do as they please without rules. And under this unspoken contract, people determine that for the sake of order and peace, they will give up a part of their freedom and decide to follow the rules and regulations of government. They elect people to represent them in the processes of government so that they have a voice in the development of these rules, and that is a fundamental basis of any government, especially a democracy. So, the power of government comes not from itself but from the consent of the governed. That is, the people agree to be regulated by government. History has proven that the minute they are not satisfied with the outcomes of that system, they can and will change it. We have seen examples of this all throughout history in the American Revolution, the French and Russian Revolutions, as well as more modern political shifts that occurred in India, the Philippines, South Africa, and Egypt, to name only a few.

One of the greatest accomplishments of the Civil Rights Movement of the 1960s is that it demonstrated that even though those who oppose justice may have some power— with their guns, tanks, unjust laws, and unfair traditions— the people have a greater power, one that reaches all the way to heaven. Fear, hate, revenge, and prejudice are all negative emotions that can serve the interests of division. They damage the ability of people to unify. When we view each other as enemies, instead of as parts of the human family who may be different or misinformed, or victimized and limited by the same oppression, then we begin to become participants in the work of separation. We become agents that enforce the hold that prejudice, hate, and division have on human societies.

We begin making decisions and acting on these ideas of in-equality and we raise our children and future generations to be-lieve these ideas. But when we begin to accept the teachings of true equality, we recognize that all things were made in the image of the Creator, so we all have kinship with everything in creation. We understand the power of the most divine, intelligent spark between us. It is this power that all of success is drawn from.

In his March on Washington speech in 1963, Dr. King put it this way: "Let us not seek to satisfy our thirst for freedom by drinking from the cup of bitterness and hatred. We must forever conduct our struggle on the high plane of dignity and discipline. We must not allow our creative protest to degenerate into physical violence. Again and again we must rise to the majestic heights of meeting physical force with *soul force*."

Soul force is the ability to counter the forces of injustice with fearlessness, knowing that your soul is connected to the greatest force in the universe. Threats, violence, and aggression are simply tools that are used to make us doubt our capacity to overcome.

We see the consequences of violence used to enforce injustice played out in the world community and on city streets every day. Many corrupt leaders, from dictators to drug lords, use fear as a means to weaken and disempower people. Fear leads us to doubt our ability to overtake someone who oppresses us, and if we have forgotten our faith we may back down and submit. We may begin to believe there is not a way out of the situation.

I remember that when I was growing up it was not acceptable for black and white people to walk on the same side of the street. If you saw a white person walking on the street who might cross your path, you were required to cross to the other side of the street. My grandmother, however, never complied with that rule. She always stood her ground and passed right by. She never crossed the street.

That refusal to bow to injustice is *soul force*, to view an owner or authority figure not as an all-powerful but as a human equal. *Soul force* implies that because this divine thread exists within all of us, it can be utilized and appealed to. *Soul force* recognizes that the "authority" figure is also imbued with this same thread. Thus, an activist can look to a higher power to imbue any oppressor with understanding, education, and willingness and light a path to the resources he or she may need.

The only reason unjust systems exist is that the masses of people silently give their consent and believe these systems are necessary—whether for their security or survival. Or we believe that is "the way things are or have to be." In other words, we believe they are the truth. Human nature is to actively defend what we accept as true. Power derives from the consent of the people and those who operate and participate in that system. The minute the people withdraw their support, these systems will collapse.

Studying an issue means breaking down all the components of change and developing strategies that can affect every aspect of that issue. If the issue requires a change in federal law, it's important to understand the jurisdiction of different branches of the federal government. Making legislative change calls for finding a voting member in the House of Representatives or the Senate and persuading that person to champion your idea inside the legislative chamber. You must make a professional presentation of your analysis of the problem as well as proposing a viable legislative solution to the problem.

That legislator will advise you as to whether your proposed bill has a chance of passing in the legislature. He or she may also identify the most likely opponents and supporters of this kind of legislation. Your role as an advocate will be to lobby other members of the legislature and talk to them about the issue, working inside channels to persuade members to vote for the bill. This work helps the legislator underscore the need for this proposal. At some point, perhaps a day or two before a major vote, the legislator may tell you that a mass protest would help her make the case that there is public support for the bill. On the other hand, she might advise you that public protest would not be prudent. Sometimes negotiations are sensitive, and controversial legislation may require discretion. Certain members of the legislature may agree to vote in favor of a bill that may contradict the wishes of part of their base. They may be able to defend this vote, if it is not cast in a public light that would raise criticism among their constituents. In these cases, protest might be damaging or might need to be toned down to hold a coalition together.

Passing legislation is an intricate process. It requires strong working relationships and a keen understanding of the legislative process, including the ability to evaluate bill language, as well knowledge of the history of similar legislative efforts. Knowing what has worked and what has failed in the past can help you craft legislation that may be able to succeed. In this country, a bill must pass the House and Senate and be signed by the president to become law. Each aspect of the process—in the House, in the Senate, and in the executive branch—has its own politics. Effective advocacy must take place in each chamber and in the White House to ensure that a federal law is passed. This can take years of persistence, the forging of many alliances, and a good deal of know-how. The Civil Rights Movement managed this intricate process successfully, and that is one reason many of its changes are still in force today.

If the change you seek occurs inside a federal agency, like the Department of Justice or the Department of Housing and Urban Development, calling a member of Congress is only a partial solution. A member of Congress can make inquiries of a federal agency on a constituent's behalf and can strengthen the force of a constituent's complaint or request by adding his influence to it. But a federal agency is under no obligation to respond to a member of Congress. As a courtesy, congressional inquiries usually receive a response, but it is not required.

If an issue calls for a judicial solution, a different kind of strategy must be employed altogether. Members of Congress are barred from intervening in judicial procedures. The judiciary is a separate branch of government, and it is not managed by Congress. Congress oversees abuses of judicial power, but that is all. It does not oversee or control the judiciary. To gain a judicial solution, a lawyer must advocate for the issue you are seeking to address judicially. Legal organizations, like the NAACP Legal Defense Fund (once headed by Supreme Court Justice Thurgood Marshall), the Mexican American Legal Defense and Educational Fund, the Asian American Defense and Education Fund, as well as the American Civil Liberties Union, litigate social justice matters. Some law firms will take on legal cases pro bono, meaning for low or no cost, if they believe the case enhances their portfolio. Lawyers must be consulted by activists to manage the judicial process. In the Civil Rights Movement, lawyers developed strategies for us that helped us get arrested, get released from jail, and ensured that we ended up with no arrest record. Our lawyers would tell us, for example, that we had the legal right to protest on the sidewalk outside the South African embassy, but once we stepped onto embassy property, we could be arrested. We would then stage a protest outside the embassy and a few individuals would decide to "break the law" and get arrested. All these elements are important to effective protesting. You need to think not only about the act of protest, but about the aftermath of a protest.

Activists must take into account Sir Isaac Newton's third law of motion, or you might call it a law of action. Newton says that for every action there's an equal and opposite reaction. That means that when activists take a stand, they must accurately anticipate the response to their action. This is one of the most important lessons you can learn from the civil rights struggle of the 1960s. We were successful in creating massive change in our society, but we did not fully comprehend the nature of the opposition. They were just as insistent as we were. As civil rights activists began to believe they had won some immutable victories and relaxed their efforts, the conservatives, many supporting the election of Richard Nixon in 1968, began engaging in strategies similar to our own.

It is important to understand all the elements of the political process to take effective action. Otherwise, you can be protesting or lobbying without impact. The Civil Rights Movement was successful because activists put together a sophisticated

strategy for protests, as well as lobbying, organizing, voter registration, voter education, sit-ins, mass meetings, fund-raising,
galvanizing high-profile support and grassroots connections,
plans for transportation, and much more. The protests were the
most visible, dramatic actions we took, but we designed all
these other strategies to develop a multi-organization, comprehensive strategy that made an impact in the end. Without craft-
ing and executing a well-thought-out action plan, long-term
success becomes haphazard and hard to come by.

When the South was being rebuilt after the devastation of
the Civil War and African American slaves were freed, amaz-
ingly progressive changes occurred in America for a few
years. The first African Americans were elected to the Senate
and the House. In 1870, Senator Hiram Revels of Mississippi
became the first black man elected to Congress. In 1875 Senator Blanche K. Bruce was also elected from the state of Mississippi. Both had been born slaves but were elected to Congress
only a few years after the end of slavery.

From 1870 to 1887, fifteen black men were elected to serve
in the U.S. Congress. By the 1890s, that number had dwindled
to five. You can imagine the sense of elation people felt, only a
few years after slavery had been abolished, to see former slaves
serving at the highest levels of government. People were in-

spired by that progress. But, at the same time, only one year after the Civil War ended many Southern state and local legislatures passed "black codes," a series of laws that allowed the government to arrest black people and send them to prison for minor infractions. So this system placed many young black men back into a different kind of slavery, still forced to work nearly for free and hired out by the state to work the fields on local plantations. These laws were implemented during the height of Reconstruction, when powerful strides were made for African American advancement.

Black codes, the rise of the Ku Klux Klan, the lynching of thousands of blacks and other minorities, unequal school systems, and the implementation of grandfather clauses and literacy tests to impede access to voting for African Americans slowed their advancement in the late nineteenth century. The Civil Rights Movement occurred almost exactly a hundred years after the Civil War. The strategies we employed secured advances in all sectors of society—employment, housing, voting, education, business, banking, science, and technology. However, just as in Reconstruction, forces immediately began taking action to limit the progress we made in the 1960s.

After President John F. Kennedy's assassination—along with the assassination of Dr. King and Senator Robert Kennedy, and serious outbreaks of violence in Detroit, New York, Newark, Washington, DC, Los Angeles, and other American cities—voters became convinced that they needed a law and order leader at the helm. Richard Nixon was first elected in 1968, only three years after the Selma to Montgomery voting rights march and the same year as Dr. King's death. The Nixon Administration launched the "war on drugs" in 1971, which began the mass incarceration of millions of blacks in America.

Also, during that period, direct action was taken against civil rights groups by the Federal Bureau of Investigation. In the 1960s, the FBI created a program called COINTELPRO, or the Counterintelligence Program, that was used to break up civil rights groups. Agents were planted in the civil rights community, many of whom became trusted members of the organizations they were surveilling. One such person, reputed to have worked with the CIA, is seen in the famous photograph on the balcony of the Lorraine Motel right after King's assassination. He is wearing a trench coat and crouching over King, while Jesse Jackson and Andrew Young are standing up, pointing in direction of the gunshots.

People claim there were federal agents allegedly traveling in the car with Viola Liuzzo when she was killed returning from the Selma to Montgomery march. We knew we were constantly being watched and surveilled. Oftentimes, our phones were tapped and our rooms were bugged. We knew that all our movements were being tracked. We often saw federal agents, stationed around the areas where we were protesting and marching, taking notes. At times we suspected that some had infiltrated our ranks. Most movement leaders had an FBI file.

I am describing these events to advise you that taking action has its price. When you protest or take action against entrenched forces of the status quo, you must be aware that action will be taken to oppose you or undermine your movement. Once you take these actions, you cannot turn back. You must be prepared. Build alliances and coalitions; do not just jump out there on your own. Consider contingencies, examine every possible outcome, and plan all the steps needed to bring about change. Devise a plan for subsequent action once change has come about that includes organizing, educating, protesting, lobbying, passing legislation, informing the people about the change, teaching them how to make beneficial use of the change, and providing for the resistant reaction to your work. Read history, study what happened in the past as you devise your plan. Just as all progressive movements are linked, so is the resistance linked.

Your opponent is not a single person, but the forces of violence, separation, and division. Recognize that people have the power to change. If people are convinced of the worthiness of your cause, soul-to-soul communication is the pathway to changing hearts and minds. Take action that demonstrates the dignity and humanity of your cause and you may find yourself the leader of an effective movement. That is the difference between a dream and a plan.

PEACE

> *"Peace is softening what is rigid in our hearts. We can talk about ending war and we can march for ending war, we can do everything in our power, but war is never going to end as long as our hearts are hardened against each other."*
> —PEMA CHÖDRÖN, *PRACTICING PEACE IN TIMES OF WAR*

We are emerging from what some historians have termed the "violent century." Several researchers have declared the last one hundred years to be the bloodiest period in contemporary history. In May of 2010, *Economist* magazine featured a cover story on a phenomenon it called "gendercide" in Asian countries like China and India, involving the killing of at least one hundred million baby girls due to the cultural belief that they are less valuable than boys. Close to thirty-three million soldiers were killed in the wars of the twentieth century. Fifty-four million civilians were killed in conflict zones, and estimates are that between eighty million and one hundred and seventy million people were murdered because of political oppression, intentional famine, and government-inflicted deaths. Some writers have dubbed the times we now live in as "the age of hate."

We think of ourselves as more enlightened, more developed than the "primitive" peoples our civilizations have supplanted, yet in all our advancement, we are responsible for more death, more suffering, more murder and mayhem than any period in recorded history. What does this say about the extent of human progress? How has our "enlightenment" failed to repudiate the transgression of violence?

Recently, I had an opportunity to visit Germany where I saw with my own eyes a solemn memorial to more than six million Jews who were slaughtered in Europe. I kept saying to myself as I walked through the horrible ruins of this crime, "How did this happen?" How could something like this have actually taken place? And how is it that today, sixty-five years after such a tragedy, we are seemingly more immune to the devastation of killing, violence, and war?

As I have reflected on my life and the intimate exposure I have had to the atrocities of hate, I conclude that the question is not who, but what. What is it about our psyche or makeup as human beings that invites us to project our fear upon one another, justify abuse to relieve our own anxieties, and then demonize the object of our ridicule? It is so strange to me that we have learned to fly in the air like birds, learned to swim in the ocean like fish, shoot a rocket to the moon, but we have not yet learned how to live together in harmony with one another.

As we look toward the unfolding of the next century, we must reflect on our legacy as a world community. Though we have bridged some of the troubled waters in the human experience that brought an end to apartheid in South Africa, the fall of the Soviet Union, and the end of hostilities in Northern Ireland, we must admit that we have dedicated a significant part of the past hundred years, either intentionally or unwittingly, to perpetrating devastation and war. We have even redefined the notion of international peacekeeping to actually mean a show of military strength. And where has this irony taken us? Certainly not into a safer world. The creation of the nuclear bomb has only resulted in the proliferation of more bombs. Its deployment as a "peacekeeping" measure did not end terror; it heightened the threat of worldwide disaster. Its looming repercussions have even emerged as the unwitting and monstrous complication of natural cataclysm, as the impacts of nuclear reactor explosions in the aftermath of the 2011 tsunami in northern Japan still haunt us to this day. Thus, our greatest fear now is that we will be victimized by the very technology and weapons we ourselves have created and attacked by the very people we trained in the methods and science of violence.

This reminds me of a speech Martin Luther King Jr. delivered, his greatest ever in my estimation. He was at Riverside Baptist Church exactly one year before his assassination on April 4, 1967, asking us to consider the spiritual cost of our promotion of death as a resolution to human conflict. He talked about his difficulty as a minister to represent the need for peace to young boys engaged in gang violence in the ghettos of the North. While he was urging them to cast aside the tools of violence, they were shooting back these words, "But what about the war in Vietnam?" And today we could add Afghanistan, Iraq, Pakistan, and Libya to the list.

———

"A nation that continues year after year to spend more money on military defense than on programs of social uplift is approaching spiritual death."
—MARTIN LUTHER KING JR.

We see today's gangbangers as abstractions of ourselves, lurid depictions of the dangers of city streets, but have we ever considered these children might mirror some aspect of our own reflection? Could it be that these young, impressionable souls, many casting about without the anchor of reasonable adult guidance, may be filling their need for direction with all the noise that surrounds them? Could they be losing their psychic innocence as they wade unprotected in streams of murky spiritual water, only to find their resting place in the seamy sewers of American life? We think the worst of them, do we not? We offer them the worst options this nation creates, do we not? And do we think it is an accident that they act out the worst in us at ever-younger ages? Could it be that through them, we are getting what we give?

Individuals and groups must judge themselves to determine whether they have abandoned any of their own responsibility. But the question for us as a society is whether we participate in any way in the corruption of the defenseless, the undereducated, and the poor in spirit. We may not be able to stop the violence of others, but we can stop our own. A child is born in innocence, and this violence does not emerge out of thin air. It is created, fomented, and nurtured in them to their detriment.

King said we are all linked in a web of mutuality, and what affects one of us affects us all. This motto applies to all that we are, not only the best within us, but also the worst. That is the true value of transparency. It acknowledges that what is done in secret, even at the highest, most secure levels, can travel across the membrane of a unified human consciousness, and be discovered. It can also invade and infect the weak-minded and the most vulnerable. That is why the first act of peace is to silence the war raging within, and once we are still inside, we have a greater capacity to assist others who are struggling with the conditions of violence.

Is it a coincidence that we have actively participated in this century of violence while our city streets are riddled with gun violence and gang war? Is it by accident that we have intruded on the lush green forests and the desert sands of foreign lands spreading the intelligence of militarism while the serenity of our countryside is complicated by crystal meth and crack cocaine? In King's speech he cited the words of a Buddhist priest who marveled at our focus on the possibilities of military victory without recognizing the "deep psychological and political defeat" we incur in the minds and hearts of the people we defend and those we are working to subdue. We are reminded of this truth daily through the bitterness and turmoil we unleashed in Iraq, Afghanistan, and the constant unrest in parts of Africa and Latin America where proceeds of war play out their ugly conclusion. We are one people, one human family, and the actions of one of us affect all of us.

Though our legacy proves violence may provide a short-term delay in hostilities, we emerge from the work of killing with questions about the true nature of honor, nightmares of mayhem, and a corrupted sense of right and wrong. The struggle does not lend itself to an evolved understanding of the power of faith, of truth, of peace. If anything we are left mourning our virtue, thirsting for truth, and longing for peace. And what we have gained is a more precise, more horrific understanding of the capacity to destroy.

These are not the values that sustain civilization, but the ones that corrode them at the core. If we were to analyze the efficacy of all the wars we have waged in this century as a precursor to peace, then logically the world should be more peaceful than ever before. Why is the opposite true?

We constantly ask how we can effectively thwart a threatening adversary with the posture of peace. But this power has been demonstrated on our own shores, yet its guidance remains invisible to us. The philosophy of nonviolence is studied and revered around the world, yet we fail to see the avenues it opens to us here at home. It was a gateway to the Arab Spring, to nonviolent change in Serbia and Poland, in Germany and South Africa. Why don't we recognize the power of what we accomplished here at home? If we can use light to heal and light to see, why not use light to secure ourselves against darkness? If we take the time, we can understand that the philosophy and strategies of nonviolence were a kind of genius that enabled even the undefended to fight back without the black arts of destruction. It taught an entire generation how to stand up without compromising their spiritual integrity and how to reform the most powerful nation on earth using methods that heal the human soul and uplift human society. If we can research the avenues of war, then we can also develop and mechanize the products of peace.

President Eisenhower warned us decades ago against feeding the enormous appetite of the military industrial complex. And since that time we have disregarded the admonition of a president and a general and proceeded to revolve our entire economy around the industries of war. If we are ever to heed Eisenhower's advice, it will mean cooperation and collaboration between nations in efforts that finally admit this world is not ours to hoard or to waste, but it can only be ours in future generations if we share it equitably among one another. That is the only way each of us can survive and thrive. We must use what we need and then protect what remains for the betterment of future generations.

This shift in priorities does not mean demonizing industry or defaming profit. Even Gandhi saw business as an aid to human advancement, and profit as a powerful incentive to create. We cannot go about shutting down the innovations of others; that too is a form of violence. But we must work together to creatively transform industry to reflect a reverence for the earth, the development of sustainable, renewable manufacturing processes, and a respect for human dignity across the globe. Instead of an economy based on the buildup to conflict, we must pursue an economic center based on the enduring power of peace. People say this seems too simplistic, too unaware of treaties and contracts, history and culture, which all create a tangle of imperatives too complex to unravel. But if we want change, we have to determine to be different. We cannot use the same excuses as before.

Once we step outside of our belief in the need for violence and mandate the way of peace, we will discover pathways we have never tried, personally, locally, nationally, and internationally. There are technologies of peace; there are the research and methodologies of peace. There are the intelligence and industries of peace. They exist; we simply have to decide to explore them. The 2010 rescue of coal miners in Chile trapped beneath the earth taught us a powerful lesson. Once we decide collateral damage to any form of life is not an acceptable outcome, it is not hard to devise means and mechanisms to preserve life rather than cast it away as though it is expendable. We already know the way; we just have to exercise the will.

As a young boy, I was determined to go to school because

I saw education as the only way out. I remember the first time I ever visited Tuskegee Institute, the school founded by Booker T. Washington, a former slave who became an adviser to presidents. I remember hearing about one of its famous professors, George Washington Carver, a scientist and inventor who revolutionized agricultural and industrial uses of the peanut. The presidents of Tuskegee were held in extremely high regard in our community, and when people talked about Frederick Patterson or Luther Foster, they seemed to stand up a little taller and speak a little bit more precisely. To this day I still feel so proud when I am driving back home to Troy. I get off Highway 85 after traveling more than one hundred miles from Atlanta into Alabama, exit on to Route 29, and within minutes I am rolling by the campus of Tuskegee Institute.

I have visited many college campuses in the four corners of this country and in the heart of the Midwest—the campuses of the Big Ten, the Ivy League, and small picturesque universities in idyllic settings around the nation. To me, there is no campus as beautiful as Tuskegee. Its wide green lawns are gorgeously maintained, inlaid with redbrick buildings, some original, some contemporary. I will never forget the first time I laid eyes on that scene. I was in the third grade, and it was my first field trip outside of Pike County. Tuskegee was like my Emerald City. It represented everything I felt that education could do. It could bestow a grace, honor, and intelligence in life that I glimpsed even at that early age, but realized was being actively withheld from me.

"Education is the most powerful weapon which
you can use to change the world."
—NELSON MANDELA

Sometimes when I was needed in the fields to help my parents pick cotton, peanuts, or corn, I would get up very early. I would get dressed and then hide under the front porch until the school bus stopped at my house. Then I would hop on the bus without my parents knowing. They were always angry when they discovered I was gone, as most parents would be, but they never punished me for going to school. We were all victims of the narrow limitations our society had proscribed for us. They were trapped too, between a rock and a hard place that required them to pit their survival as sharecroppers against the education of their children.

As a child, I was restless to escape the boundaries that had been set for me. My soul was calling me to do something, to take some kind of action to burst the seams of this agricultural captivity. It was protesting, loudly declaring that I was greater than the confinement I was being forced into. I was struggling against this reality the only way I could, like a bird in a cage that has had a chance to see the sky. And I was not alone. Most of us were frustrated by the truncated quality of our lives, but we had no idea how to change it.

My parents' strategy was to work within the strictures set for them, and they succeeded in ways that elude many of us today. My father bought three hundred acres of land by scrimping and saving a measly, unfair salary. On that land sat a larger home for his family, a chance for some margin of independence. He raised nine children who all became responsible citizens. Others shook the dust off their feet and left the South to live in New York, Chicago, Washington, Los Angeles, and other cities only to find bondage of another kind.

If you were lucky or your parents had enough resources, a college education could open some doors. It did not mean you were free of the limitations of racial bias, but it gave you more options in a limited field to accomplish great things, like the men of Tuskegee I had heard so much about. And then there were always a few who simply gave up and gave in to anything that would help them forget the odds against them. These were my options. We had no money for college, leaving my family was out of the question until I got much older, and working in the fields for a lifetime seemed like a form of punishment to me.

You cannot imagine the sense of awe, the sense of relief I felt when I heard the voice of a young Southern minister, not too much older than me, who was openly discussing the injustice that no one dared to address. He told us it was our Christian duty to take a stand against problems in our society. Martin Luther King Jr.'s words were the blue sky this restless bird needed to fly. They were the candle illuminating a darkness threatening to swallow us all up, and they lit a path to a clearing where we could stand up and be the men and women we were born to be.

We realized that the violence all around us offered an uncommon opportunity to perform a great spiritual work. We began as outcasts reserved for condemnation and scorn, but we were transformed into a shining army of peace moving in the center of God's love. We were rescued from the outer limits of human existence to become philosophers and priests, leaders and advocates, shepherds and witnesses to the way of truth. And in these new roles, we cut a path to a new America. We discovered that our dignity, and in fact all human dignity, was not tied to the way we looked or how we dressed. Our dignity was not related to the size of our wallet or the digits in our zip code. We discovered that it did not matter how we were judged by mankind, our own souls were imbued with the power to work miracles to change water into wine, the meek into the mighty, to change base metal into pure gold.

In the South, we knew our adversary would stop at nothing to silence our activism. We knew we could never match his readiness to annihilate our resistance. So we ceded him that ground and challenged him instead to defend himself against the work of loving peace. Our simplicity outwitted his complex system of rules and regulations. Our quiet insistence exposed his comfort with brutality. Our numbers robbed him of an ability to minimize our opposition. As our singing rejuvenated our spirits, it left him seething in frustration. We learned that we could be warriors of peace who rejected the short victories of destruction for struggles that made us victors in this world and the next. Our peace exposed the moral condemnation of violence, and it brought a nation to its knees.

Despite our desire to do no harm, there are still casualties in a conflict fought with the weapons of peace, but the human cost and the spiritual toll does not begin to compare with the deficit of war. Too few talk about the walking wounded of the movement. Carolyn McKinstry was also just a little girl who had just passed the bathroom where four girls, her friends, were killed by a bomb that went off after Sunday school in Birmingham. That day defined her life. She said she spent twenty years moving through a career, marriage, and family suppressing the pain of that day. In her retirement, she became a minister and today she shares the story of what she experienced to heal the hurt and to hopefully ease the tensions of today's flirtation with racial violence and separatism.

And there was another poignant survivor that day. So few people realize there were actually five girls in the bathroom. The four girls who died are very well known, but one, Sarah Collins Cox, the sister of one of the four who was killed, survived. When I hear her speak today about the incident, in that same sanctuary of the First Baptist Church in Birmingham, her voice is haunting. She had been washing her hands at the facebowl on the opposite side of the bathroom, when her sister asked her to help tie the sash of her dress. She looked back in her sister's direction and before she could move toward her, the bomb exploded. Shards of glass tore through her eye. She climbed through a hole in the wall to the street and was bleeding from her nose and ears. Today she is blind in that eye and is facing the possibility of blindness in the other. There is no anger in her voice. Her soft, wistful words acknowledge nothing of her struggle, but I hear the legacy of pain when she says, decades later, "I never knew whether she ever got to tie her sash."

Oh yes, there are casualties of nonviolent struggle, but

they are far fewer than in a violent war. And the casualties are suffered on the side that has prepared to bear the blows in peace. I don't think I ever heard that any of our offenders suffered a single physical loss. And that is as it should be, because the real battleground is on a higher ground, in the heart and in the mind where love and truth will be the final victors. And it is not because of protests, but because of this struggle of conscience that the consciousness of this nation has been transformed.

We were soldiers of a nonviolent revolution, a revolution under the rule of law, a revolution of values, a revolution of ideas that changed America forever. But we carry few scars from the battle of peace because we never violated one human being in our conflict. The believers in peace never raised one finger in anger. We never wounded another human soul. We did not even bruise the ground we stood on to bring this transformation forward. Some of us still struggle with psychological turmoil, after wading through the breathing fire of hate. Flashbacks of images burned in our minds of the twisted, jeering mouths and the hands that would harm still leave some of my colleagues in a cold sweat, but these horrors were not compounded by the damage of war. And even these difficulties can be healed by the values of nonviolent struggle. Those walking wounded still have the ready philosophy of love and forgiveness to heal any injury that lingers. Instead of thousands of college-aged soldiers who lose their limbs and their youth in a crisscross of gunfire, only a few of our soldiers were wounded and even fewer were killed. The warriors of peace lived to profit from the new openness their courage ushered in. A few suffered, struggled, and died so that millions could find their way toward peace.

How many deaths will it take? How much war must we visit upon ourselves before we recognize that war does not work? War is bloody; war is messy. It not only tends to hide the truth, but to sacrifice the truth. War postpones the unalterable need to reconcile our actions to our knowledge of the truth, whether they are the actions of nations or of single individuals.

War that is waged for power or dominion over other human beings obscures the inevitable truth that we are all members of one family, and no matter who has conquered whom, who now resents whom, who holds bitterness against whom, the only way we can have true peace is to set aside our injuries and our dedication to revenge and accept our equal divinity. Martin Luther King Jr. said that peace is not the absence of tension, but the presence of justice. It is not the cessation of war that brings peace; it is justice that brings peace, even in the midst of struggle.

To most of us peace is a noble ideal, a worthy goal of human endeavor. Who would argue that our world would be vibrating at a higher level if we were to find a way to end violence and war in the Middle East, to eliminate ethnic cleansing in the Sudan, to stop conflict rape in the Congo, to end the drug wars in Colombia and Mexico? Yet somehow, though we all would say we want peace, in our own lives and in our own world, we view it as a distant star, something we say we seek but never expect to truly gain. Gandhi would tell us there is no way to peace. Peace is the way.

If we are ever to be the same leaders in the work of cooperation as we are in the work of domination, we will have to face the truth about ourselves, about our lives, and about our legacy as a nation. Nonviolence is confrontational. It is not silent in the face of injustice, but "creatively maladjusted" to the problems and conditions of this world. If you truly want peace, you cannot be satisfied, apathetic, or compliant with the hypocrisy of the status quo. You must follow where the truth leads, because at the end of that road lies the cessation of struggle—true peace. This means refusing to deny or resist what our soul insists is true and serenely acquiescing to the goodness of what is truly real. Once we accept the truth that is aligned with the order of the universe, all conflict will cease. And until we accept the truth, we will writhe in the pain of resistance to what will be. Until we see truth manifested in our world and in our way of life, we must confront injustice with the power of peace to clear and cleanse violence, anger, and animosity from the human condition. Sometimes you have to be willing to turn things upside down to make them right side up.

This reminds me of an elderly woman named Mother Pollard who was asked to share her feelings during the height of the Montgomery Bus Boycott. The boycott lasted over a year, and it required her and many others to walk long distances to work. She was old, and she may have been tired, but she said something like, "My feet are weary, but my soul is at rest." In her seventy or eighty years, she had never seen more turmoil around her, never seen more controversy, rumor, and commotion than during the boycott, but her silence in the face of injustice disturbed her more than any upheaval the boycott could ever have created. All those years riding that bus, she was sitting down. She was still, but she was not at peace. The boycott turned things upside down, but for old Mother Pollard they had been made right side up. Her feet were weary, but her soul was finally at rest.

The way of peace and nonviolence is not the way of the weak. It takes courage to face the truth of your condition or the condition of our society. It takes courage to admit that we are not living up to our ideals of freedom and justice as a people. It takes courage to admit that we participate in killing, violence, and hate around the world. And once you face the truth, it is difficult to retreat back into a state of unconsciousness. Becoming aware of the truth requires action, and that is when the struggle begins.

Struggle is the act of making things right. It is an effort to encourage change in the affairs of humanity or the affairs of one's daily life so they will conform to a new awareness of the truth. And that struggle is an expression of the inner dissonance a person experiences within his or her own mind and heart, a continuing disturbance that will not cease until the circumstances have been corrected. The stress associated with this disquietude was alluded to by Mother Pollard, who found her only peace inside the turmoil of struggle. Why? Because she was finally able to take some steps to correct the wrong she had been required to participate in almost her entire life.

The struggles of humanity will not be corrected in a day, a week, a year, or even a generation. Those of us who are active participants in the struggle must recognize that we are part of a long line of activists who have come before. Some stand next to us in the struggles of our time, shoulder-to-shoulder partners in the midst of conflict, and there are others who must follow after us in order to finally overcome violence with peace in human affairs. Where will we stand in this continuum of struggle? Each individual participates in this conflict whether he or she is actively or passively engaged. The divine spark that is resident in each of us challenges us to be the light and stand up for what is right. We can decide whether to obey the call of the spirit or abide in denial, confusion, or hostility to the truth. But once we have heard the voice calling us to act, we cannot rest until we do something. And it is when we find the courage to act on that calling that we can finally begin to find peace.

"If you want to make peace with your enemy, you have to work with your enemy. Then he becomes your partner."
— NELSON MANDELA

Many have asked me whether I was afraid when I was standing on the Edmund Pettus Bridge, looking out at a sea of Alabama state troopers. They seem bewildered when I tell them I was not afraid. I was at peace. It did not matter that I was looking down the barrel of a gun or an army of guns. It did not matter that troopers were on horseback ready to fire tear gas. It did not matter that citizens had been deputized and were carrying every weapon they could find.

I had long before accepted that I might die in a protest, and when I saw those troopers, I realized my time might have come to an end. But that was all right with me because I knew deep within my heart that I was living the life I was meant to lead, and I was willing to follow that calling wherever it took me. If I had to die, I believed my sacrifice along with the sacrifice of others would mean something. I had made peace with the understanding that if I died on that bridge, I would have offered my life in contribution to an effort that was larger than myself. My life and my death would have served a divine purpose, to liberate a people and maybe even a nation. I could think of no greater gift I could give to humanity. My soul was at peace with whatever the outcome might be. I had faced the truth of my circumstances. I made a choice not to abide in the deep disturbance of a silent, segregated South, but to find peace in the midst of a mighty wind that turned things upside down to make them right side up.

As I was working on this book, I realized the condition of humanity at this time led me to speak more about the need for peace than peace itself. I challenged myself to find a moment when I witnessed the peace that I hope to see in the world today. I always marvel at the progress we have made in the South that has encouraged so many people to return. The fear that hung heavy in the air is gone, and people move much more freely today than in the days of my childhood. That is not to say the struggle is over in the South; it is definitely not. There is still discrimination and injustice in the South and across this nation, which must be addressed, but those of us who lived through the '40s and '50s in America know we have come a long way.

I can say I have witnessed the advent of greater peace in our society, but that is in comparison to all the turmoil I have seen. I wanted to find a moment in contemporary history that others with different experiences might be able to point to, a place where the tension and strife in our society had ceased, even temporarily. I looked for one moment that we may all remember, a moment that expands beyond politics or partisanship, but expressed the ability of a nation to heal. For me, the nomination of Barack Obama as a candidate for president and his inauguration in Washington represents a brief glimpse at the power and potential of peace.

There was a radiance about America then, a great coming together of so many people, races, generations, and beliefs. For one brief moment in our history, we found a way to put down our strife against one another. For a few days, weeks, and months all the false reasons we use daily to look down on others, to separate ourselves from one another, fell away, and we opened our hearts to the kind of equality that our founders envisioned but did not have the courage to create. In that moment we decided to face the truth of our oneness with one another, and when we did we experienced the beauty of peace.

The night of Obama's nomination at the Democratic National Convention felt like what we would have called a "happening" in the sixties. Our jubilation moved beyond the pride of a political win. I had never seen anything like it in all the political conventions I have ever attended. There was a great feeling of release, like we were glad as a nation that we had finally done it. It was one moment in our long history where we sensed the possibility of liberation from all the pain and struggle of hundreds of years. It was as though the hearts of the people and a nation were ringing together, shouting, "Free at last. Free at last." The commensurate confetti suddenly seemed so appropriate, the applause felt more authentic, and there was a lightness in the air, an ease, and a comfort I have never felt at a convention before. It was only an evening, only one night in all of our history, but it reminded me so much of the way we felt in the movement, like a band of brothers and sisters, who accepted the truth of our own oneness. At that moment, we were at peace with ourselves as a people and as a nation.

The day of Obama's inauguration was bitterly cold, one of the coldest I have ever seen in Washington. It was below freezing, but that did not stop the people. People came from all across the country, sleeping on cots and sleeping bags on the floor in the homes of families and friends some of them had not seen for years. Some started walking miles away from the National Mall in Washington to be there on time. For many, it was their first visit to the capital city and definitely the first time they ever had any desire to attend an inauguration.

We all felt invested in what we had created. We felt we all had had a hand in something great, in opening a door to a new day in America. Party affiliation did not matter. Race, color, and nationality did not matter. We set all our differences aside, and we huddled together warming ourselves in the generosity of one another on that very cold day. We lowered all our barriers, all our resistance, and we joined as one nation. People were sharing blankets to stay warm on the mall, helping strangers navigate the crowds, making room for people they would not normally even acknowledge. If you remember that day, if you were there or at home watching, maybe you felt it too. Maybe you felt a nation and a people who put aside their judgment of one another for one moment to share in the comfort of peace.

The international community also reveled in that time, perhaps even more than we. They were with us. They abandoned their mounting anger toward us. They put aside all the damages done, and they shared our joy as a world community. I think that is why they saw fit to give President Obama the Nobel Peace Prize. That award was an indication to those who were familiar with our turmoil for over four hundred years that we had finally turned a corner, that we were finally willing to lay aside the vestiges of slavery and expose ourselves to the radiant sun of real freedom. It also meant that if we could do it, maybe they could do it too. Maybe they could release their burden of violence and revenge. If we could do it, maybe the French and the Algerians could learn to live together. The Germans and the Turks could learn to peacefully coexist. The Italians and the Greeks could put aside their grievances. The Serbs and the Croatians could lay down their division. Maybe even Israel and Palestine could finally admit their kinship. Maybe on every continent, in every nation, in every corner of the world people could put their long-standing grievances aside and decide to live in peace. The Nobel committee was saying in effect: If the United States can move beyond the tension of hundreds of years of human slavery and the bloodshed of the Civil War, then maybe, just maybe, the world community might find a way to finally lay aside the ancient struggles of the past and move to a new level of human existence.

At that moment, we glimpsed a few seconds of what our future could be. We felt in this country a flash of the true joy and freedom of living in a Beloved Community, living in a society based on simple justice that values the dignity and the worth of every human being. There is a great deal of work left to do on the road to peace. I stand with His Holiness the Dalai Lama, who has said we have a chance today to live in contrast with the past, to bring an end to the Age of Violence and make the next hundred years the Age of Peace. It is my hope that we will turn our attention to the truth of mutual cooperation, the truth we must ultimately come to accept, as well as the healing and the compassion that will build a better world. We can do it. We must do it. Gandhi would say it is either nonviolence or nonexistence. And Martin Luther King Jr. would say we must learn to live together as brothers and sisters or we will all perish as fools.

I ask you to reach down inside yourself, and find the truth your life is compelling you to see. That is your road to true peace, and it is the beginning of the evolution of humankind. Because every change in the world starts within. It begins with one individual who envisions his or her micro-universe the way it can be, and settles for nothing less. And as one individual moves toward the light, that light ignites more individual flames and eventually the revolutionary inner work becomes a transformative outer work that builds into a bonfire of light, the kind of light that can change the world. It starts from within, with one individual who seeks the way of peace. Will you be that person?

LOVE

"We are all bound by the ties of love . . . Even as there is cohesive force in blind matter so much must there be in all things animate and the name for that cohesive force among animate beings is Love."
—MOHANDAS GANDHI, *YOUNG INDIA*, OCTOBER 6, 1921

Love is the willingness to sacrifice, to be beaten, to go to jail, to be killed for the betterment of society rather than live out your life in silence. The Civil Rights Movement, above all, was a work of love. Yet, even fifty years later, it is rare to find anyone who would use the word love to describe what we did.

We were consciously aware that unity was our ultimate goal, and if that was truly our aim, we had come to grips with the fact that after all the warring was done, reconciliation, love, and forgiveness would have the final say. Our protests were our way of standing in the truth to reach our errant brothers and sisters and encourage them to see the abiding truth that was there before the foundation of the world and would last beyond our existence—we are one people, one family. I like to use the analogy of one house to describe our kinship to all humankind. We all live together in the same house—in different rooms, perhaps, but under the same roof and within the same walls. If one section of our house begins to rot—a basement, a back room, a closed-off closet—the entire structure is in danger of collapsing. It is only by recognizing our unity that we can prevail.

In 1961, thirteen original Freedom Riders, seven blacks and six whites, left Washington, D.C., traveling on a Greyhound to New Orleans. We sat in an integrated fashion on the bus to test a Supreme Court ruling that rendered segregation in interstate transportation illegal. Although this new law had been passed, states in the Deep South continued racially discriminating, forcing blacks to sit in the back of the bus and to surrender their seats to standing whites. Most bus stations still posted WHITE WAITING and COLORED WAITING signs. Our plan was to challenge this injustice. Typically when a train or bus traveling south from New York City, for example, would get below the Mason Dixon line, the black passengers would be asked to get up from their seats and move to the back of the bus. Our plan was for black and white Freedom Riders to simply remain seated next to each other. And when we got off the bus and entered the stations, white riders would use restrooms marked COLORED and black riders would use restrooms and facilities marked WHITE. It was that simple, but I knew the farther South we traveled, the more likely we would be to run into violence. No matter how bad the beatings were we would not physically fight back. Ours was a nonviolent mission. We knew it was dangerous, and all of us wrote out our last requests before we boarded the bus in case we did not return. On the Freedom Ride, I was prepared to die.

All of the participants on the ride had been taught the discipline and philosophy of nonviolence, but those of us who participated in the Nashville movement had benefited from gifted teachers—Rev. Jim Lawson, himself a conscientious objector in the Korean War who had traveled to India to walk in the footsteps of Gandhi, and Rev. Kelly Miller Smith, a learned and esteemed church leader in Nashville. They taught us the philosophy of Gandhi, Thoreau, Emerson, Plato, Aristotle, and others to illuminate the lineage of thinkers who believed in the inalienable rights of humankind. We had also participated in role playing that prepared us mentally and physically for this moment.

We left Washington and rode through Virginia and North Carolina without much disturbance until we hit Rock Hill, South Carolina, on May 9, 1961. My seatmate was Albert

Bigelow, a nice, white gentleman from Connecticut. Albert got off the bus first and was immediately besieged by violent attackers. Then I got off the bus and tried to enter the bus station, walking into a so-called "white waiting room." I heard, "Other side, nigger," as I tried to pass in front of a group of angry men standing near the door. Instantly, fists were coming from everywhere punching me in the face. I was knocked to the floor and repeatedly kicked in my sides. Albert and I were left in a pool of blood. Some police officers approached us, asking if we wanted to press charges against the men who had so savagely beaten us, and we said *no*. They were flabbergasted. They could not believe it or understand why. We simply told them that ours was not a struggle against individuals. It was a struggle against a system of injustice. We got back on the bus and kept pressing on.

May 20, 1961. Though we had been forewarned of possible attacks, there was an unusual calm as the bus approached the terminal in Montgomery, Alabama. That peace was short lived. Within moments, an angry white mob descended, brutally beating us with our own suitcases, dragging us out of the terminal as we tried to take cover in cabs. They had baseball bats, chains, bricks, and any weapons they could find. There is a famous photograph of me and another rider, Jim Zwerg, standing together, splattered in blood after the attack. With blood on the sleeve of his jacket, Zwerg has a tissue in one hand while he feels the hole where his teeth had been with the other. I doubt that professors who teach the history of the movement today would say that if you boiled down our intent into one all-encompassing residual word the remaining essence would be *love*.

Yet I am here to tell you that among those of us who were at the heart of the movement, who fully imbibed the discipline and philosophy of nonviolence and viewed it as a reflection of profound truth, for those of us who accepted it not simply as a tactic but as a way of authentically living our lives— our sole purpose was, in fact, love. We would settle for the proceeds of justice and equal rights, but the force guiding our involvement was the desire to redeem the souls of our brothers and sisters who were beguiled by the illusion of superiority, taken in and so distorted by their false god that they were willing to destroy any contradiction of that faith. If we were pawns of an unjust system, they were also so complicit in their own degradation that they justified wrong as a service to the right.

The inequities that surrounded us in school, sharecropping systems, housing, and land ownership were justified by a belief in the subhumanity of the oppressed. Because people believed certain members of the population were incapable of elevating their minds or their station in society, it was easy to see slavery or sharecropping as a beneficent system that was offering savages more than they could ever achieve on their own. Lynching and vigilantism were considered duties, the necessary protection of men who were guarding the sanctity of social boundaries and the "purity" of their lineage.

No matter the rationale, these ideas put a virtuous face on centuries of brutal history that actually robbed our aggressors of their moral grounding and made them creative participants in violence. Though these oppressed were not responsible for the original distortions, our complicity with their abuse helped to verify the validity of these injustices. But the minute we stopped participating in a degrading system, it gave those who were troubled by nagging questions and those who were too blinded to see any hypocrisy a door, a window out of a way of life that was bound to deteriorate around them. Being willing to withstand their rage, to serve as a reflection in which they could see themselves, was actually an act of compassion and love that helped release millions of white Southerners from the burdens inherent in the work of hate.

You may easily say that self-love is another evident spiritual derivative of what we accomplished. Without a doubt, that is true, the capacity to stand up at times when we would have once been afraid was deeply empowering. To be able to count ourselves among the few willing to die for a just cause was ennobling. There is no question that reviving our own sense of self-worth was perhaps a subconscious draw for every participant in the movement. It also became a clear benchmark for the ministers and teachers who prepared in us a willingness to sacrifice our own lives, if necessary, for a cause. A kind of elegant dignity coupled with the simplicity of our protest was a part of the movement's attraction to those who flooded into the South to stand with us. People wanted to do something in the face of this injustice. They longed for the profound sense of pride that accompanies righteous activism along with the need to fulfill a greater purpose. The Civil Rights Movement gave people something tangible to do so that they could actively contribute and participate in creating a unified nation.

To reconcile ourselves with one another, we must release our judgments and make peace with the fact that we are one. This country was founded on the ideal that we are all created equal. If we truly believe in the equality of all humankind, how can we put down and belittle one another? How can we disrespect and prejudge one another? How can we come to the point where we malign and hate one another?

For those who could not find their dignity in the actions of nonviolent resistance, especially after the assassination of leaders like Dr. Martin Luther King Jr. and incidents like the

Orangeburg Massacre in South Carolina, black power or the ideas of self-defense grew in popularity. They were advocated as quicker paths to self-respect and an appreciation of one's self-worth through retaliating against the wrongs brought against us. It may have worked for some people. I would never question the value of affirming oneself, or recognizing and utilizing collective strength to make our voices heard. However, I would say that the danger of matching threat for threat, violence with violence, resistance with force, is that it has the potential to create the same spiritual deficit the victim is struggling against within him or herself. The notion of an eye for an eye, though biblical, only lowers an individual to the level of his or her attacker.

We see this played out so dramatically in the plague of war. Our stated intention in Iraq, for example, was to rescue the Iraqi people from tyranny. Yet, after the tyrant was deposed and killed, we replaced one form of violence—a human dictator who reigned through fear—with another. The people of Iraq are still not free from fear today, despite the claims that they are better off now. Because we used the same tools as the violator, the truth of the situation is obscured, making the victims defending themselves begin to look strangely similar to the aggressors they are defending against.

This is also played out on the streets in gang warfare. Gangs often form as an attempt to defend against marauding bullies. However, the way these new gangs choose to protect their own people is to carve out territory, bear arms, wear different colors, and settle disputes with weapons. The motivation for self-defense alone morphs into the same violent marauding that began the difficulty in the first place. And there are spiritual consequences for this bitter work that an individual cannot defend against. Young boys and girls develop hardened attitudes. They grieve the violent deaths of friends and family members. Some turn to drugs and alcohol to obscure the nagging of the soul. Darkness cannot overcome darkness, only light can do that. Violence can never overcome violence, only peace can do that. Hate can never overcome hate, only love can do that.

If the act of nonviolent confrontation redeems the dignity of those who engage in it, how is it that an action of love has the power to redeem the perpetrators of violence? Our implacability grounded in love was ultimately what disarmed the weapons of fear and thwarted the intention of our violators to annihilate us. In order to beat people who radiate love and acceptance, an individual has to override his or her own conscience and allow anger and brutality to have its way without limitation. Most people cannot do this. They have a conscience. Their souls convict them of the injustice they are about to inflict, and they hesitate. Sometimes, that moment of hesitation creates a self-awareness that bars them from acting.

"No one is born hating another person because of the color of his skin, or his background, or his religion. People must learn to hate, and if they can learn to hate, they can be taught to love, for love comes more naturally to the human heart than its opposite."

—NELSON MANDELA, *LONG WALK TO FREEDOM: THE AUTOBIOGRAPHY OF NELSON MANDELA*

Diffusing the fury of violence by obstructing and redirecting the intention of an attacker is itself an act of love. Violence has consequences. My colleague Rep. Spencer Bachus from Alabama, who represents Birmingham today and lived through the days the city was called "Bombingham," often discusses how merciful nonviolent confrontation was, even for those engaged in hate, because it spared Birmingham decades of revenge killings that he believes would have been the aftermath of a violent confrontation. Having compassion for your attacker means you harbor no malice and seek no retribution for the wrong that has been done. It is an offering of love that asserts the victim's self-worth. It makes room for the inner working of his or her soul that has a way of invoking a quiet insistence to do what is right.

This brings to mind the one and only attacker, of the forty times I was arrested and jailed, who apologized to me for his actions. Almost forty-eight years after that now famous Freedom Ride stop in Rock Hill, South Carolina that left Albert Bigelow and me so badly bruised and bloodied, Elwin Wilson, one of our attackers, wanted to come to meet me.

Wilson had apologized to other Freedom Riders during ceremonies honoring them in South Carolina and had mentioned his wish to find the men he had beaten up that day in Rock Hill. I welcomed him to Washington and as we sat, Wilson looked deep into my eyes, searching my expression, and said he was the person who had beaten me in Rock Hill in May of 1961. He said, "I am sorry about what I did that day. Will you forgive me?" Without a moment of hesitation, I looked back at him and said, "I accept your apology." The man who had physically and verbally assaulted me was now seeking my approval. This was a great testament to the power of love to overcome hatred.

Each and every one of us has the power to turn our enemies around because we are all a spark of the divine. It does not matter whether we are fit or weak, short and scrawny, or big and strong. There is no adversary who can defeat us if we believe in our own inner capacity to overcome. Sometimes we have to gain tools to overcome our adversaries. We might need to study, to get help, to pray, or develop a plan, but there is no obstacle we as human beings cannot overcome.

"Not all of us can do great things. But we can do small things with great love."
—MOTHER TERESA

From the moment he attacked me that day, this former member of the Ku Klux Klan and I had entered into a strange bond. Though we were linked through an act of hostility, the connection was made nonetheless. Even in violence, the unity of humanity cannot be broken, and that is why it is more productive to acknowledge the bond from the beginning and move from there. The struggle is simply an elongated path to the abiding conclusion: We are all one people, one family. Wilson has said publicly that he is glad to be able to count me as a friend today, and he has expressly mentioned his gratitude that we did not press charges that day. His life and the life of his family could have been changed forever if South Carolina had actually tried and convicted him. But beyond that, had he been tried, it would have added a layer of justification to the rationalization that always accompanies guilt. If he had been publicly vindicated, which would have been the likely outcome, it would have been more difficult for him to come to the point where he eventually believed an apology was in order, and more difficult for him to feel love.

Elwin Wilson also said that he was glad we did not have any weapons that day. If Albert Bigelow and I had inflicted harm in Rock Hill, we would have fueled the flames of violence instead of putting them out. Any sense of remorse would have had to compete with the fire of anger. Instead of a possible reconciliation, revenge would have been the product of that violent confrontation in Rock Hill. But because we met this man in love and offered him our respect despite his obvious hatred, it gave him nothing to justify his anger. He left that day only to review it in his mind so many times over the years. The resonance of our innocence made room in his own soul for the realization that he needed to ask for forgiveness. I was surprised to hear him clearly restate forty-eight years later the essence of what I had said to the police officer as I declined to press charges almost half a century earlier: "We're not here to cause trouble. We're here so that people will love each other." That was how he put it. The impact we left was undeniable.

What Elwin Wilson did took courage. He could have

simply made amends in his heart, but to publicly put aside his differences and admit his error is unique and bold. By doing this, he demonstrated so poignantly for all to see that love that opens its arms to help heal the pain of another's suffering—not violence in self-defense—has the power to ultimately disarm the attacker, preserve his or her integrity, and enable the truth to do its work. Love that meets the separating action of violence with forgiveness affirms that our ultimate and eternal unity is transformative. Even as I walk the halls of Congress and pass my Republican colleagues, some of whom have proposed some of the most damaging legislation I have ever read in my entire career, I often say, "Hello, brother." It is an acknowledgment that though we seem to differ today, in the end, after all the struggle is over, love will be the only result.

There is no more convincing invitation for atonement than an awakening or a realization that occurs in one's own soul. The nonviolence of the movement was an act of love because it enabled an entire society to awaken to the truth of human unity. It made it easy for a nation to finally see the wrong was not only in the law, but in us. And it gave us the chance to work on correcting it. There is no question that there is more work to be done as a nation to indicate our full embrace of this understanding, but because the movement did not inflict damage, it allowed a healing to take place. It allowed this nation to take another powerful step toward the ending of its inner turmoil.

Once hostilities cease, warring parties begin the work of living together, determining how to resolve their differences—even the problems that instigated the conflict in the first place. Nonviolent action stands on the truth of the unity of all humankind, and it sees the offending party as a brother or sister who has gone wrong. Its participants exercise their right to noncooperation with unjust law or incorrect principles, but they always remember the humanity of the offender, knowing that eventually balance will be restored and the two will have to find a way to come together again.

Forgiveness plays a powerful role here because it paves the way for reconciliation and love. In the movement, we did not seek retaliation or revenge against our attackers, because we recognized that we could not harm them without harming ourselves. We saw them as wayward brothers and sisters who had lost their way. We learned to visualize them as innocent babies. No child is born in hate. All children are born in hope, love, and innocence. It is a troubled world that teaches these vicious values. We saw that our attackers were also victims, victims of a negative indoctrination that taught the false values of superiority and inferiority, the sanction of violence and brutality, and the justification of inhumanity and hate.

Instead of suggesting that people with cultures and customs we do not understand, people with different color skin, or those who speak another language are somehow beneath us, instead of developing an elaborate rationale to justify our discomfort, it is more honest to simply admit our insecurity and gain acceptance.

Once we accept differences as an acquiescence to the truth, wisdom begins to emerge. Perhaps the variations in appearance and expression that seem to occupy so much of our concern—tall, short, black, brown, straight hair or curly, white or yellow, fat or slender, gay or straight—are more an expression of the broad imagination of the Creator than they are an indication of our value or worth. If these manifestations of love are all equal, then they are merely expressions of the infinite possibilities in the universe.

Once we accept the perfection of other human beings and the limitations of judgments based on our own experience and understanding, interestingly enough, our perspective broadens. Our minds open to the deeper nature of perfection. We see that perfection is not merely a mirror of what we have seen, known, and loved, but it reflects a multiplicity of different realities all based on one central concept: the unity of us all.

The goal of our work in the movement, of all of our activism, and our protest was to come to love. Our desire was not a temporary victory. We did not want to throw loose dirt on a shallow grave. We wanted to push and pull and do all we could to permanently end the injustice of legal segregation and racial discrimination, and we defined those problems in broad terms. That is why there was a strong relationship between the Labor Movement and the Civil Rights Movement, between the struggles of post-Holocaust Jews, Latino farm workers, the poor, the sick, the disenfranchised, and the disabled. We saw all of these struggles as linked to the same root cause, and we wanted to do all we could to defend the dignity of humankind, no matter what form of oppression people were facing.

Today, young people have no comprehension of how we could have taken what seems to them to be such illogical and irrational steps in the fight for freedom. They cannot understand how sitting next to another human being or drinking from the same water fountain could be viewed as illegal. The work of love left no scars, no obscuring of what side was right and what side was wrong. The only damage that needed and still needs healing is that inflicted by unjust laws and evil traditions, but as a society motivated by the power of faith, love, and peace, we took the necessary steps to move in that direction.

Inside this discipline and philosophy, I became grounded in an unshakable way. Sometimes I feel like a tree planted by the rivers of water. A tree that is deeply rooted cannot be easily moved. Hurricanes and tornadoes can bend its branches almost down to the ground, but it takes a great deal to unseat a tree that is firmly planted. I know today that there is a power, a force that can never be corrupted or defiled. And that power is love. Roots of love nurtured by a river of faith are a sure protection against many dangers, even the power of military might. And I say this not as an idealist who speaks in poetry and platitudes, but as a realist who has faced an army of weapons drawn against me with love as my only defense.

The love we are able to feel toward one another today across communities and cultures, even though it may only be a trickle from a dam that still needs to be released, cannot be easily shaken. Some people want to turn back, but it will not be easy to turn off the spigot and retract the waters that have flowed into human hearts so easily. That love is so much closer to the truth of who we really are as a people and as a nation than we have ever been before. And that love is here to stay. The more we focus on it and live in its truth, the greater our light will shine as a nation, the more enlightened our policies will be. Creative diplomacy will supersede the robotic drone of militarism, and we can find our natural place as leaders in a world community that has rejected the illusion of separation and responds with the power of love.

RECONCILIATION

This little light of mine, I'm going to let it shine.
—HARRY DIXON LOES

Why do we struggle? Why must we, as members of the human family, immerse ourselves in the agency of turmoil and unrest to affect the evolution of humankind? Why participate in the work of justice at all? Why risk beating, torture, even death to sacrifice ourselves within the network of our family, on our jobs, in our communities, the nation, or the world at large for the sake of progress we may not live to see? Why must we be the ones? Each of us must answer those questions according to the dictates of our conscience and the principles of our faith. I believe that we are all a spark of the divine, and if that spark is nurtured it can become a burning flame, an eternal force of light. I believe the true destiny of humankind is to recollect that it is light and to learn how to abide in infinite awareness of the divine in all matters of human affairs.

Thus, the true mission of our work in government and through community action is to help free humanity to follow this high calling. That is, in essence, what the Founders of this nation wrote within the heart of the Constitution, that government must not impede the divine right of human beings to be guided by the whisperings of their own souls, to seek the path that magnifies, actualizes, and incarnates the beauty of their individual flames. The freedoms we are guaranteed—to worship, to gather together, to speak freely, to publish our unfettered criticism and comments, and to seek the remedies of collective imagination (or government) to aid us in resolving our problems—were mandated to provide maximum room for growth led by the dictates of the spirit.

The Declaration of Independence expresses the purposes of human community by affirming this as a fundamental root of our founding: "We hold these truths to be self-evident, that all men are created equal, that they are endowed by their Creator with certain inalienable rights, and among these are life, liberty, and the pursuit of happiness." Inalienable means that no law, no man, no woman, no child, no power can separate us from this divine quest.

THUS, OUR PURPOSE while we are here, in the most basic sense, is to be a light that shines—to fully express our gifts so that others might see. When they witness our splendor, when we show them it is possible to shine radiantly even in the darkest night, they begin to remember that they are stars also, meant to light up the world. And if we are brilliant, like a Bobby Kennedy, a Martin Luther King Jr., a Jim Lawson, or a Fannie Lou Hamer, then the intensity of our flame can light the path of freedom for others. We can be way-showers, light-bearers, and mentors of the light who encourage others to flourish, create, manifest, and glow. As each person turns on the illumination of the spirit, revealing gifts, talents, and visions for the future, we can blend our majesty in a glorious concert of communion. We can burn as one unified sun that can light up our world and even our universe. This planet can smolder with imagination, burn with creativity, reverberate with love, oneness, and peace. The infinite is possible, but this beauty can only manifest through us.

LET ME BE clear. This work is not mandatory. We can choose to block our own perception of the light and live in darkness. In fact, we can become so dark that even our eternal spark becomes very, very dim, so faint that we are hardly aware of its existence. Yet, more often than not, no matter how tarnished or weak the flame, when the forces of darkness seem like they are about to consume us, we will ourselves to survive, and we begin to stand in the center of our inner light and invite its power to clear away the darkness that has clouded the soul.

As ASPECTS OF one Creator, we have the ability to define the world around us, so the center of our will becomes our reality. Together through our thoughts and our deeds, we create the conditions of our habitation. When we set our minds against one another, when we focus on destructive energy and propagate the negative notions of separation, division, discrimination, rejection, domination, and war, we waste our power in a futile attempt to debase, degrade, and even destroy the light in others. This is a misappropriation of our energy and a depletion of our inner resources. That is why war does not work, why hatred is a burden, why putting others down cannot free us. It is only a way to hide from the light that we must ultimately perceive as the workings of the divine in an orderly universe. Our condemnation of others only delays the coming of that day when we finally understand we must put our strife aside and awaken to our true union with one another, no matter how different we might believe one another to be. And when we accept ourselves as brothers and sisters, we come into a new understanding. The majesty of Creation opens to us, and we begin to perceive the vastness of the universe, the infinity of human possibility, and the expanse of the power that resides within us.

When we follow the path of light, we co-align with the most dynamic forces of the universe, and we become greater than the sum of our parts. As we marched across the Edmund Pettus Bridge that lonely six hundred joined with a host of silent, unseen holy witnesses who marched with us. Though we were rejected, condemned by mankind, shunted off into some dark corner, we remembered our inner worth, and we began to shine. All we needed was the courage to march to demonstrate the power of human dignity, and the spirit that is within all of us did the rest. Because we chose to emerge from the oppression of darkness, our sacrifice helped to usher in a great transformation. This is the power we stood upon in the movement. This is the message of Gandhi, of King, of Thoreau, and so many others who have passed and of those to come: This light can never be defeated. You must use it and show the world its beauty.

ALL OF OUR struggles here are based on one erroneous, pervasive, and persistent belief that we are somehow separated from the divine, that some of us have more light than others, therefore making them more deserving than others. We believe some people are more special, more beautiful, more capable, more influential, more intelligent, more gifted, and have a greater capacity for good than others, often based on material possessions and outer appearances. At the root, that is why we are engaged in a struggle now in the Congress led by one group of people who truly believes their role is to defend the privileges of the elite. They defend tax breaks for the rich and ask for trillions in cuts to the safety nets that protect the middle class, the elderly, the sick, and the poor, because, in essence, they believe one group is more important than the other, more deserving than the other, and one contributes more good than the other. This is actually an illusion that is blind to the interdependence of the entire creation, which unites the weak with the strong, the privileged with the poor, and the ugly with the beautiful. All of the inequities of our world are basically attempts to actualize this erroneous belief. And that is why there is turmoil, because we are in conflict with the truth, working to manifest an idea that is false.

The Occupy movement, the Arab Spring, the Civil Rights Movement, the activism of Gandhi, the French Revolution, and other social transformations down through the ages came to pass because people decided they deserved to live under a higher conception of reality. They decided they deserved better. They deserved more good than the ideas their contemporary society afforded them. They experienced the insufficiency these impoverished concepts create, and today's activists are reading the writing on the wall, formerly obscured by some policies of government and aggressively pursued by multinational corporate interests. The message they read and summarily reject suggests that 99 percent of the people should serve the interests of 1 percent, to use the Occupy terminology. Over years, decades, and even centuries of injustice, the people have had to bear many attempts to dim their light, to rob them of their inalienable rights, but ultimately the truth prevailed. Potted down to a flicker, in danger of annihilation, the people began to call on the power within them to push back the darkness, and as one light began to shine, others followed suit. A movement began to roll through the land based on the people's affirmation of the truth.

It is the responsibility, yet the individual choice, of each of us to use the light we have to dispel the work of darkness, because if we do not, then the power of falsehood rises. Through our inaction it becomes stronger, and a more potent force. It can even lead to the dimming of the light of all humanity born on this planet. That is why we struggle. That is why we fight to contribute to the confirmation of what is good, to seal our compact with love within our own lives and within our world. Through our work, our prayer, and our successful over-coming we ground the light on this planet. Just as Gandhi made it easier for King and King made it easier for Poland and Poland made it easier for Ireland and Ireland made it easier for Serbia and Serbia made it easier for the Arab Spring, and the Arab Spring made it easier for the protests in Wiscon-sin and Occupy Wall Street, so our actions entrench the power of the light on this planet. Every positive thought we pass be-tween us makes room for more light. And if we do more than think, then our actions clear a path for even more light.

That is why forgiveness and compassion must become more important principles in public life. We say we are a be-lieving nation, yet when we are wronged, the people demand revenge. If we truly believe, then what is the role of forgive-ness, mercy, and compassion in public life? Could it be that those who had the power to save Troy Davis's life, those who had the power to stop our march to war in Iraq, those who could offer mercy to the drug addicted, the AIDS in-fected, or a second chance to prisoners, are not afraid of politi-cians, law, or government, but are afraid of us? Could they be afraid of the people who shout for condemnation, punish-ment, revenge, of those who want to spill blood for blood, ravage an eye for an eye, or rip out a tooth for a tooth?

Living as light means putting away remedies based on

fear, retribution, and revenge and acting collectively through government to respect the dignity of all humankind—not just those we agree with or whose paths we understand—but every human being. It means that if correction is necessary, we must search for ways to rehabilitate that are consistent with our faith. We cast out the sins of war, torture, terrorism, corporal punishment, and condemnation and find ways to bring individuals back into balance through remedies founded in truth. Then our ways and means will not lead to turmoil, but will turn us back toward peace.

All our work, all our struggle, all our days add up to one purpose: to reconcile ourselves to the truth, and finally accept once and for all that we are one people, one family, the human family, that we are all emanations of one divine source and that source is Love. Our struggle to affirm the light despite oppression, depression, conflict, poverty, hunger, disease, violence, and brutality is a loving gift we give to ourselves and one another to help humanity move toward the day when we can readily separate the light from the darkness and the equal incandescent beauty of the light that is in us all.

You are a light. You are *the* light. Never let anyone—any person or any force—dampen, dim, or diminish your light.

Study the path of others to make your way easier and more abundant. Lean toward the whispers of your own heart, discover the universal truth, and follow its dictates. Know that the truth always leads to love and the perpetuation of peace. Its products are never bitterness and strife. Clothe yourself in the work of love, in the revolutionary work of nonviolent resistance against evil. Anchor the eternity of love in your own soul and embed this planet with its goodness. Release the need to hate, to harbor division, and the enticement of revenge. Release all bitterness. Hold only love, only peace in your heart, knowing that the battle of good to overcome evil is already won. Choose confrontation wisely, but when it is your time don't be afraid to stand up, speak up, and speak out against injustice. And if you follow your truth down the road to peace and the affirmation of love, if you shine like a beacon for all to see, then the poetry of all the great dreamers and philosophers is yours to manifest in a nation, a world community, and a Beloved Community that is finally at peace with itself.

ACKNOWLEDGMENTS

I would like to thank Gretchen Young at Hyperion, who believed in this project from the beginning and guided it through to success; Bob Barnett, whose wise counsel helped to bring this idea to fruition; Brynda Harris in the Library of Congress (LOC) Office of Congressional Relations; the entire staff of the LOC Office of Facilities Services; and the librarians of the Jefferson Reading Room at the LOC, who made a home for my collaborator while she was on sabbatical working on this project. I thank Julie Siegel, Maureen O'Neal, and Allyson Rudolph for additional work on this project. There are two people without whom this book would never have been possible: Brenda Jones, one of the best communications directors I have ever had the pleasure of working with, an extremely gifted writer who has so often taken my ideas and given them life; and my chief of staff, Michael Collins, a faithful leader who has guided this project through all of its challenges into safe harbor.

I would also like to thank all my teachers, without whom I would have been like a bird without wings. They showed me how to fly. I would like to thank the Reverend Jim Lawson, a mystic and a master teacher in the way of nonviolence, and the Reverend Kelly Miller Smith, for his foresight in perceiving the value of nonviolent discipline and starting those classes in the basement of a church decades ago. I would like to thank all those great souls who participated in the nonviolent struggle for social change in America and those known and unknown who gave all they had for the cause of justice.

And, above all, I would like to thank Martin Luther King Jr., for being willing to serve all of humanity as the embodiment of the power and the imperative for nonviolent transformation. Without him, I do not know where I would be today.

Thank you to all those in the struggle who made a difference that enriched our past and those who will make a difference in years, ages, and eras to come.